Achievement
ENGLISH

CHRIS CULSHAW

OXFORD

UNIVERSITY PRESS

Oxford University Press, Great Clarendon Street, Oxford OX2 6DP

Oxford New York
Athens Auckland Bangkok Bogotá Buenos Aires
Calcutta Cape Town Chennai Dar es Salaam Delhi
Florence Hong Kong Istanbul Karachi Kuala Lumpur
Madrid Melbourne Mexico City Mumbai Nairobi Paris
São Paulo Singapore Taipei Tokyo Toronto Warsaw

and associated companies in
Berlin Ibadan

Oxford is a trade mark of Oxford University Press

Achievement in English © Chris Culshaw, 1999
Published by Oxford University Press 1999

All applications to perform this play should be addressed in the
first instance to the Permissions Controller, Educational Division, Oxford
University Press, at the address above.

A CIP catalogue record for this book is available from
the British Library

ISBN 0 19 833765 5

Printed in Singapore by KHL Printing Co. Pte Ltd.

Contents

Introduction

Why *Achievement in English*?	Because it will help you to do just that: achieve better grades in English.
What's in the book?	The book is made up of eight units. These can be tackled in any order. Each unit is rather like a ladder. The first activities are fairly easy. The later ones are harder.
Will it help me to pass my exams at 16+?	Yes. The book deals with some important examination themes like advertising, leisure, television, poetry and story-telling.
What kinds of topics does it cover?	A wide variety including *Coronation Street*, *Macbeth*, love poetry, radio plays, computer games, video nasties, sports reporting and children's toys.
Will this book improve my reading skills?	Most of the activities require careful reading and rereading, and that's the key to improving your reading. There are also some timed reading targets for you to have a go at. These will help to develop confidence in your reading.
How?	If you recognize whole words – like your best friend's face – you don't have to puzzle over them – like a stranger's face. The more words you recognize the faster you read. If you have to slow down and sound words out, letter by letter, then you lose confidence.
In what other ways will this book help my reading?	It will help you to learn to read 'between the lines'. This is a key skill. Very often there isn't one answer to a question. You may be asked for your opinion on a topic. There may not be a 'right' answer to the question. Two people may react to the same poem, for example, in very different ways.

What about my written answers?	A lot of the activities will help you to extend short written answers, so that you can show the thinking behind your answer. This is important in an exam. If you learn to read between the lines, then your written answers will show that improved skill.
What kinds of speaking and listening skills will I be using?	In every unit there are discussion tasks, but a lot of the activities pose open-ended questions which you may want to discuss. For example, the influence of violent videos on children.
I've seen this symbol **2** in the book. What does it stand for?	This indicates a speaking or listening activity.

SHOPPING

Sales talk

···················· **ACTIVITY** ····················

1 Complete these phrases, using the words below.

a Prices slashed! 20% _____ all prices
b While stocks _____
c Offer must _____ Friday
d Delivered to your _____
e Special _____
f Allow 7 _____ for delivery
g Money back if not _____
h UK _____ free
i No _____ extras
j _____ 7 days a week
k P+P _____
l Please _____ an sae

send	included	days	offer
door	last	postage	off
hidden	satisfied	open	end

KEY: **2** This symbol indicates a speaking or listening activity.

2 Which phrases:
  a tell you about the price of the product?
  b tell you about postage costs?
  c tell you about delivery?
  d try to persuade you to send off for the goods today?
3 Design a mail order advert for these roller blades.
  Include information about cost, postage and delivery.

On your bike

Bicycle Stall, Accrington Market, c1905

ACTIVITY

1 Are these statements true (T), false (F), or not enough evidence (NEE)?

a All the bikes on the stall are black.

b Some of the bikes are second-hand.

c One of the stall holders is a woman.

d All of the bikes on show cost about £12.

e One of the bikes on the top of the stall is a ladies' bike.

f There are no children's bikes on display.

g Some of the bikes do not have mudguards.

h All of the bikes have the same size frame.

2 You are the owner of the 1905 bike stall. You travel by time machine to a modern bike shop. Use some or all of these words to describe what you see and think:

shock	surprise	choice	colours
shiny	shapes	sizes	lightweight
safer	faster	clothing	equipment

A modern bicycle shop

Phone lines

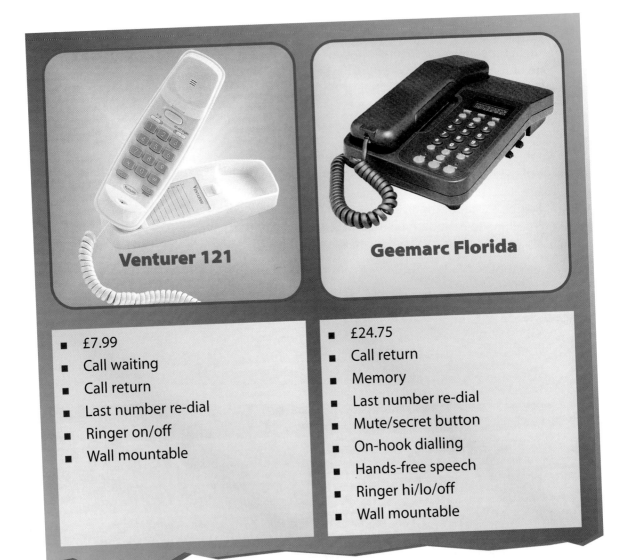

Venturer 121

- £7.99
- Call waiting
- Call return
- Last number re-dial
- Ringer on/off
- Wall mountable

Geemarc Florida

- £24.75
- Call return
- Memory
- Last number re-dial
- Mute/secret button
- On-hook dialling
- Hands-free speech
- Ringer hi/lo/off
- Wall mountable

ACTIVITY

1 Use the table on page 11 to help you answer the following questions.
If you have a Venturer phone will you be able to:
- change the volume of the ring?
- know the number of the last person who called?
- fix the phone onto the wall?

2 If you use a Geemarc phone will you be able to:
- know who is calling before you answer the phone?
- automatically dial the last number you called?
- dial a number without picking up the receiver?

Features on modern phones

Call waiting	Lets you know someone is trying to call you even when you are speaking on the phone.
Call return	Lets you know the number of the last person who called.
Caller display	Lets you know who is calling you before you pick up the phone.
Ring volume control	Lets you adjust the volume of the telephone ring.
Memory	Lets you store numbers that you use a lot.
Last number re-dial	Lets you automatically dial the last number you dialled.
Mute/secret button	Lets you speak to someone in the room without letting the caller hear.
On-hook dialling	Lets you dial without picking up the receiver.
Hands-free speech	Lets you talk and listen without lifting the receiver.

.... **EXTENDED ACTIVITY** ....

3 Pick one of the people below. List 3 phone features they would find useful and say why:
- a parent looking after a very young baby at home
- an elderly person living alone
- a young person starting a small business at home.

Toy story

Barbie's new wheelchair friend

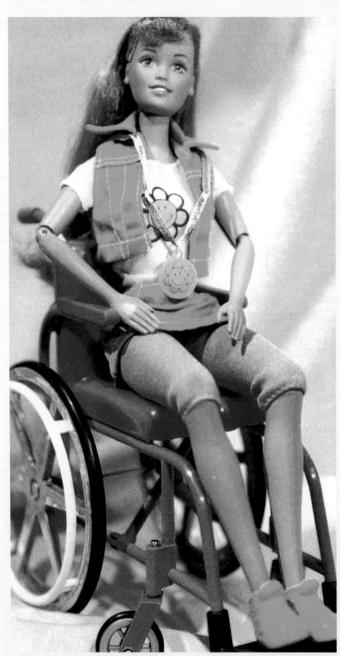

A DOLL in a wheelchair has gone on sale in the Barbie collection.

Barbie's new friend Becky is intended to change attitudes about people with disabilities, say makers Mattel.

The strawberry blonde doll costing £12 comes in a pink wheelchair, and is dressed in a green outfit and a white shirt. "Barbie's world reflects the real world. Barbie has African-American friends. She has Asian friends. She has Hispanic friends," said Mattel product manager Marla Libraty. Becky is currently only available at Toys 'R' Us stores in the USA.

The Express
22 May 1997

ACTIVITY

1 Why did Mattel decide to make a doll in a wheelchair? Pick the best answer from the four below. Give reasons for your choice.

a Lots of kids have friends with disabilities. So lots of kids will buy the toy.

b Becky is unusual, and kids like unusual toys.

c To change the way kids think about people with disabilities.

d To show Barbie is kind and likes Becky even though she has a disability.

2 You have a young niece. She is 8 years old and a wheelchair user. She collects Barbie dolls. Would you buy her Becky? Give reasons for your answer.

EXTENDED ACTIVITY

3 Do you think Mattel will make a friend for Ken, who is a wheelchair user like Becky? Give reasons for your answer. Try to use some of these words in your answer:

male	masculine	active
strong	fit	attitudes
action	ability	disability
image	sales	stereotype

Sing it to me!

Background

Jenny is the assistant manager of a large record store. CC is the interviewer.

CC   What sort of products do you sell?

Jenny   CDs and tapes mostly, but we also sell T-shirts, posters, videos and games.

CC   Which are your best selling items?

Jenny   CDs and tapes. But we sell a lot of posters, and video games have really taken off. We sell a lot of T-shirts too, but mainly in the summer.

CC   What kind of T-shirts?

Jenny   Mainly pop, especially if a group has a number one hit. Then we sell out within the week. Films too. We sold loads when Trainspotting was on in town.

CC   What do young people buy from your store?

Jenny   We get lots of school kids in, mainly on Saturday morning.

CC   What are they looking for?

Jenny   They might buy a couple of singles or a poster. They spend about a fiver. Pocket money, I suppose. It's TV that drives these sales. And the media. If the kids see a group on TV, or in the teen magazines, they come in looking for that. We have to be sure we have hundreds of copies. Once a hit song takes off, it really flies. We sell hundreds in a day.

CC   Do you promote hit singles in a special way?

Jenny   Yes, they have to be up front, so you see them as you walk in. We always display loads of copies. We fill up six or ten racks with the same CD cover. So kids will think 'That must be popular.'

CC   Do you target young people in any other ways?

Jenny   We use an in-store CD which has all the new singles on it. We play this every day, at 12 o'clock and 4 o'clock.

CC   Why?

Jenny   We get lots of kids coming in during lunch-time and after school.

CC   What about the future?

Jenny   I think we'll see the death of tapes. Everything will be on CD. CDs are expensive, but I think they will come down in price. Who knows? Something new might come along.

CC   What do you like best about your job?

Jenny   It's interesting and fast moving. There's always something new coming along. It's a great job if you're interested in music, and I am. You have to know a lot about music – all kinds of music, not just the charts. It's hard work. But it does have its lighter moments. Sometimes people come into the shop looking for a particular record. If they don't know the title I say, 'Sing it to me!'

ACTIVITY

1 What do these phrases mean:
- video games have really taken off
- it's TV that drives these sales
- once a hit song takes off, it really flies
- they have to be up front
- we use an in-store CD
- the death of tapes?

EXTENDED ACTIVITY

2 If you were the manager of a record store, how would you target young people? With a partner, make a list of ideas. You could use some ideas from the interview, as well as your own. Pick one product (CD, poster, T-shirt, etc) and say how you would promote it in your store. Use drawings/diagrams to illustrate your answer.

EASY LISTENING
BLUES . FOLK
COUNTRY

15

Getting it right when it goes wrong

Background

Sometimes when you buy something, like a CD player, it does not work. Then you take it back and complain. There is a law called the Sale of Goods Act. This will help you to get things put right.

The Act says that goods must be:

- ► 'of satisfactory quality': this means that it must not be damaged or faulty.

- ► 'as described': this means that it must be the same as the description on the packet or in the advert.

- ► 'fit for all their intended purposes': this means it must do what the packet or advert says it does.

  Adapted from *Young Citizen's Passport, the Citizen Foundation,* 1996

Waseem bought a watch. When he put it on, the strap fell off. He took it back to the shop. He got his money back. He told the shopkeeper, 'This watch is not of satisfactory quality.'

a Kate bought a watch. The shopkeeper said it was waterproof. Kate wore it to go swimming. It filled up with water.

b Kerry bought a walkman. When she played her tapes on it, the volume was so low she could not hear the music.

c Louise bought a pair of jeans. The label said 28 ins waist. She measured them and found they were 32 ins.

········· ACTIVITY ··········

1 Role play what Kate, Kerry and Louise should say when they complain. Use words from the Sale of Goods Act, as Waseem does.

With reasonable care

Background

The law also helps you to put things right if you get poor service. The Supply of Goods and Services Act says that service must be provided:

▶ 'with reasonable care and skill'
▶ 'within a reasonable time'
▶ 'at a reasonable charge'.

Young Citizen's Passport

a Abbie's bike needed a repair. The woman at the bike shop said it would take two days. Abbie went back two days later. The bike wasn't ready. Abbie had to wait two weeks before her bike was fixed.

b Julie's shower was leaking. The plumber fixed the leak but he cracked three tiles in her shower when he did the repair.

c Chris broke a wheel off his rollerblade. He took it to the shop to get it fixed. The shopkeeper told him a new wheel would cost £5. The shopkeeper charged Chris £15 to fix it.

········· ACTIVITY ··········

1 What did the three people on the left say when they complained? Use words from the Supply of Goods and Services Act.

2 Describe another situation involving faulty goods or services. Write down what you will say when you complain.

Oi, what are you looking at, Dummy?

The mannequins in Selfridges' windows have caused a bit of a stir this week.

Their heads turn from side to side. Their eyes open and shut. And they talk for hours on their mobile phones.

But then, these dolls are human. For this week only, the posh store in London's Oxford Street is experimenting with a new concept in window-dressing.

Eight real people live in the large display windows, leading aspirational lifestyles in the luxurious lounge sets. Everything they wear, read, eat or drink is available in-store.

They're getting £250 – with tea breaks every 90 minutes – just for 'chilling out.'

It's a tough job, but someone's got to do it. So I decided to spend a day as a not-so-dumb dummy.

"Just do what you do at home," I was instructed by Paul Chambers, Selfridges' head of creative design. "The aim is to sell merchandise with style and energy just by being you. We want people to think they are being a fly-on-the-wall in your beautiful home. They will be captivated."

Stumble

Captivated? By little old me, swigging my tea, reading The Mirror, watching telly, eating lunch, phoning my mates? Hardly captivating stuff.

But to my amazement, the bargain shoppers, businessmen, tourists and foreign students meandering down Oxford Street seemed fascinated to stumble across me getting on with my mundane life, seemingly oblivious to the world outside. They just can't help stopping to gawp.

As the sun pours in the window, I stack the state-of-the-art Bang & Olufsen CD player, pour a little designer mineral water into a matching designer glass, fluff the sheepskin rug, plump the Moroccan tapestry cushions and stretch out idly on the sumptuous, 12ft white leather sofa.

Suddenly there's a tap on the window. "Smile, please, for the camera," a fat American bellows, as she squashes her brood together for a souvenir snap.

As people close in on my goldfish bowl to scrutinize me, I start to feel a bit like an art exhibit. I try reclining motionless for several minutes, then reach for a glass of water, making a party of teenage schoolgirls run away shrieking and squealing.

A toddler in a pushchair just smiles knowingly. I've confirmed what she has always suspected: mannequins can come to life. We exchange waves.

"What are you doing?" shouts a woman, hammering angrily on the glass – just when I was coming to a good bit in my book.

I lunch on sushi with chopsticks (£5.95, The Food Hall).

My spectators hang on my every mouthful and applaud when the raw fish eventually lands in my mouth.

A frustrated British businessman can't understand why I'm just sitting there. He wants me to do something. I make a phone call but he's still not satisfied. He suggests I remove an item of clothing.

Mercifully, the police respond swiftly to my call and cart him off to Soho.

After that, people keep banging on the window, trying to make me laugh. It's all rather wearing.

By the end of the day, I can't wait to abandon my temporary luxury des res and rush off home to my modest little East End terrace. And be alone.

Carol Aye Maung
The Mirror, 17 April 1997

ACTIVITY

1   Use a dictionary to find the meanings of these words:
    a   mannequins
    b   concept
    c   merchandise
    d   captivating
    e   gawp
    f   sumptuous
    g   scrutinize.

2   How many people were employed to be dummies? How long did they work and how much were they paid?

3   Why does the writer say that she wanted to spend a day as 'a not-so-dumb dummy'?

4   What does the American tourist do after she taps on the window?

5   Why do the teenage girls run away shrieking?

6   Sum up, in your own words, what the writer felt about her day in her 'goldfish bowl'.

EXTENDED ACTIVITY

7   Role play an interview between you and a shop manager who is looking for a shop-window dummy. Make up some questions that both people might ask at the interview.

8   You get the job and spend a day in the window. Write about your day. Use the following plan:

Paragraph 1 Describe the furniture and other objects you would like in your window.

Paragraph 2 Describe what you would do to pass the time.

Paragraph 3 Describe what happens when a friend or relative sees you there.

Crash

Rail crash at Purley, removing the debris

A difficult rescue following the Clapham rail disaster

The Clapham rail disaster

4 Choose one picture and write a short newspaper report about the crash. Use your headline from Question 1 and add the following details:
- time
- date
- place
- type of train(s) involved
- possible causes
- number of casualties
- the work of the emergency services.

ACTIVITY

1 Make up some headlines to go with each picture.
2 Which of the two Clapham photographs would you use with a newspaper report of that crash? Give reasons.
3 How is the Purley photograph different from those taken at Clapham?

If it feels right ...

Background

Martin Wyness is a photojournalist. Every year, he goes to the horse fair at Appleby in Cumbria where hundreds of Gypsies meet to buy and sell horses.

THE FIRST THING I think about when shooting a subject is: "What will be the consequences for the people in my photographs? How will my work affect their lives? Could it have a negative effect? If so, should I still go ahead?"

The camera is a very powerful tool. I try to use it with respect, and with responsibility. My rule is: "If it feels right, it probably is." If I stick to that rule, then usually my photographs work – enriching everyone, including the subject.

The Appleby Horse Fair project was a 'social documentary'. I wanted my pictures to help people to

GLOSSARY
enriching – making better
ethnic minorities – small groups of a different race, within a larger group
negative – bad
reception – welcome
subject – person or thing photographed

have a better understanding of the Gypsies. I believe the more we know about ethnic minorities like the Gypsies, the less we will fear them.

I go to Appleby every year, so I have made many friends there. It is always a delight to work at the fair. Gypsies love to be photographed. They often thank me, especially if I photograph their children.

A stranger can go into a gathering of caravans and just join in. The Gypsies won't greet you like a long-lost friend. But you will hardly ever be made to feel unwelcome. I don't think I would get the same reception if I just started taking photographs on a housing estate or in a leafy suburb!

Martin Wyness, Photojournalist

ACTIVITY

1 What does Martin mean by, 'the camera is a very powerful tool'?

2 Why does he like working at the Appleby fair?

EXTENDED ACTIVITY

3 You are a photojournalist. You have been asked to take some pictures for an article on under-age drinking in your local area. Make a list of people and places you would photograph. Write about some of the problems you might have taking these photographs. Who would see them? What effect could they have? Try to link what you write to your answer to Question 1.

Sent off

A Two off as Evans men are checked

Background

On Wednesday 16 April 1997, Everton played Liverpool. The result was Everton 1– Liverpool 1. Towards the end of the match, two players, Fowler from Liverpool and Unsworth from Everton, were sent off.

B Fowler rocks Anfield's hopes

C ALL-OUT WAR

D Ferguson foils Liverpool as Fowler is sent off

G Liverpool Star out of Title Battle after Red Card

E FOWLER SHAME

F MERSEYSIDE SHOWDOWN

···················· **ACTIVITY** ····················

1 Which headline says that more than one player was sent off?

2 Why do you think the reporters use the words 'war,' 'showdown' and 'battle'?

3 Which headline is the most critical of Robbie Fowler? Give reasons.

4 Which do you think is the best headline and why?

5 Write a new headline to go with the picture.

Did he or didn't he?

Here are extracts from the match reports in four national newspapers.

A   '...the England striker threw out his arms at David Unsworth.'
'...aggressive words became punches...'
'...an ugly and dramatic end...'
The Independent

B   '...Fowler flew at his opponent and punches appeared to be
   exchanged...'
Daily Mail

C   '...a high octane clash...'
'...the burly Unsworth sent Fowler crashing to the floor'
'...Fowler flipped...'
'...the referee saw the punch-up and took action...'
The Mirror

D   ' ...Robbie Fowler's foolish frenzy...'
'...Fowler responded to the challenge with a flurry of punches...'
The Express

GLOSSARY

burly – well-built
flurry – a sudden whirling gust
high octane – likely to explode

ACTIVITY

1 Why does one reporter call the Everton player, Unsworth, 'burly'?
2 What have the phrases 'Fowler flipped' and 'Fowler's foolish frenzy' got in common? Comment on the reporters' choice of words.
3 One reporter seems to be unsure about what led to the sending off. Which one? Give a reason.
4 Why do sports reporters sometimes make mistakes? Think of other sporting events where accurate reporting might be difficult. Give reasons.

What's going on?

Background

How do we find out about what's going on in the world? This survey shows how people in the UK get world news and local news. (NB Figures do not always add up to 100% as 'don't knows' are excluded.)

World News	1985	1990	1996
Television	62%	69%	68%
Newspapers	23%	18%	19%
Radio	14%	1%	8%
Talk to people	1%	2%	1%
Teletext	0%	0%	2%
Magazines	0%	0%	0%

Local News	1985	1990	1996
Television	16%	21%	32%
Newspapers	55%	51%	41%
Radio	14%	10%	13%
Talk to people	11%	12%	10%
Teletext	0%	0%	1%
Magazines	1%	1%	1%

ITC Research, 1996

ACTIVITY

1 What is the biggest change in the way people get world news between 1985 and 1996? What might have caused this change?

2 What is the biggest change in the way people get local news? Why has this happened?

3 In 1996, how do most people get news of local events? Do you think this will change in the future? Give reasons.

EXTENDED ACTIVITY

4 Give reasons why these **local** newspaper stories might be reported in **national** newspapers or on national TV:

a Blind girl wins high jump in school sports

b Local butcher in food poison scare.

Can you believe it?

Background

The bar chart below shows how many people believe what they see or read in various media.

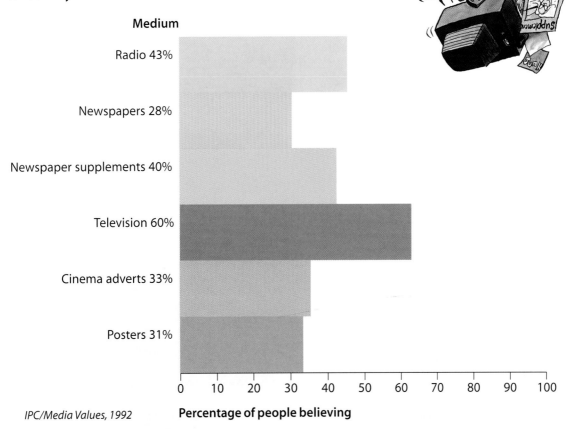

Medium

Radio 43%

Newspapers 28%

Newspaper supplements 40%

Television 60%

Cinema adverts 33%

Posters 31%

0 10 20 30 40 50 60 70 80 90 100

IPC/Media Values, 1992   **Percentage of people believing**

ACTIVITY

1 Which medium is most likely to be believed? Why do you think people believe in this medium more than the others?
2 Which is the least likely to be believed and why?
3 Pick another medium from the survey and give reasons why people might not trust this.
4 If the survey had asked: "Do you trust your local newspaper?", what do you think people would have said? Give reasons for your answer.

EXTENDED ACTIVITY

5 Ask 5 or 6 people in your group how they find out about local news and events. Do they get their information from newspapers, radio, TV, or friends? Compare their answers with the information given on page 26.

Human interest

AN ARROW ESCAPE

Bow ordeal Nat keeps smiling

Young Nat Spink was rushed to hospital with a 3ft arrow sticking out of his stomach...and still found the courage to smile.

Nat, 12, was lucky to escape with his life,
5 when he was accidentally shot by a pal in a park.

The home-made bamboo shaft, tipped with a rusty six-inch nail, lodged just above his navel.

10 Paramedic Lindsay Osborne, who was in the ambulance that took Nat to hospital, said yesterday: 'The arrow was quite close to major blood vessels and vital organs. Had it gone any deeper it could have pierced them.'

15 At the hospital, doctors tied the loose end of the arrow to a light fitting above Nat's bed while they decided best how to remove it without further damage.

And yesterday Nat was back home in
20 Totnes, Devon, with his mother Dot, 45. She said: 'His best friend had made this bow and arrow out of bamboo and fish line. Without thinking, the arrow was fired. It wasn't at close range. A couple of other kids
25 moved out of the way.

'But Nat didn't. It was a sheer fluke and bad luck. It was a totally innocent act.' Nat said: 'The arrow was going through the air and I said 'It's going to hit me.' The next
30 thing I knew it was in me. I was screaming 'Aagh, it's in me'. Dot said: 'The doctors used a scalpel to cut the bamboo but he still had the nail in him.

'He needed a general anaesthetic before
35 they sorted him out and cleaned up the wound.

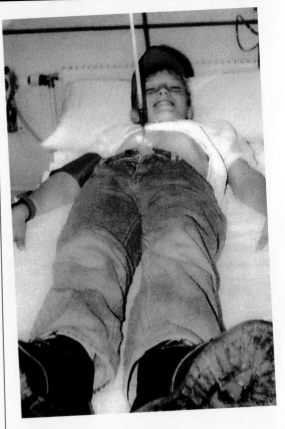

'There are no stitches. The wound will close naturally.'

She added: 'We hope this will be a lesson to others. It could have been so much worse.'   40

The *Mirror*, 8 October 1997

GLOSSARY

anaesthetic – drug that puts patients to sleep for an operation

innocent act – act done without meaning harm

navel – stomach

vital organs – heart, lungs, etc.

ACTIVITY

1 How was Nat hurt? Who is to blame for the accident? Give reasons.

2 Which facts tell you that Nat was in real danger?

Paper boy finds baby abandoned

A NEWSPAPER delivery boy told yesterday how he found a new-born girl abandoned in bushes during his morning round.

5 Police began a search for the baby's mother following 13-year-old Darren Simm's discovery at 8.30 am in Newcastle upon Tyne.

Darren said he was on his bike when he heard a baby crying. He stopped and 10 discovered the child, wrapped in sheets and a towel, next to a fence in the Whickham area.

Darren said: 'If I hadn't been doing my round this morning I wouldn't have found 15 her and she would have died.'

The baby was taken to the maternity unit at Queen Elizabeth Hospital, Gateshead, where she was found to be suffering from the effects of cold but 20 otherwise all right.

Darren, a pupil at Whickham Comprehensive School, said: 'I was riding along the road on my bike when I heard a baby crying.

'I stopped and looked around for a few 25 seconds and then saw something next to the fence near a bush.

'It was moving backwards and forwards so I went and got my mum. We came back in 30 the car and when we realised it was a baby, my mum picked her up and we took her home.'

Police later carried out house-to-house enquiries on the nearby Grange Estate. 35

Acting Inspector Dave Bone appealed to the mother to contact the police. He said: 'She may be in need of medical attention and we would ask her to please come forward.'

40

The Scottish Herald,
27 December 1996

ACTIVITY

1 Which facts tell you that the baby was in grave danger?
2 Give reasons why Darren might not have spotted the baby.
3 Which of the two stories has the best headline and why? Make up new headlines for both stories.
4 If you were the editor and had to choose to print just one of the stories, which would you print and why?
5 There is not enough space for the complete stories in your newspaper. Reduce one of them to the key facts (about 60 words).

EXTENDED ACTIVITY

6 Pick one of the stories, and write down the questions the reporter had to ask to get the facts.
7 Write a follow-up to that story, a year after the event.

Emergency!

Background

At 4.20 pm on Wednesday 5 November 1997, an airliner made an emergency landing at London's Heathrow Airport. This is how the event was reported on Channel 4 News at 7 pm. This report was the third item in the programme, taking up 5 minutes of a 40-minute broadcast.

Channel 4 News Report

Jon Snow, news reader (*live in the studio*): There is major disruption at Heathrow Airport tonight after a Virgin Atlantic plane made an emergency landing when part of its landing gear failed to open. Passengers on the airbus from Los Angeles were immediately evacuated when the plane skidded across the runway. Ten people were slightly injured as they left the plane. Lindsey Taylor has the latest details.

Lindsey Taylor, reporter (*voice over*): The Virgin A340 airbus, similar to this one, had flown from Los Angeles with 98 passengers and 16 crew when it developed problems with its landing gear. Only the right-hand undercarriage appeared to have deployed.

Rob Seabrook, eye witness (*voice over, caption on screen telling the viewer who is speaking*): You could see the wheel-bay was still shut, the left-hand side, I believe. The right-hand wheels were down, but the others weren't.

Lindsey Taylor, (*voice over, picture of plane*

landing at Heathrow): Pilots receive
regular training for just such emergency
landings. According to an eye witness, it
was carried out with great skill.

John Asher, eye witness (*voice over,
caption on screen*): He held it off the
ground for as long as he could. He
reduced the speed to a minimum. As it
touched down it was one-sided and it hit
the runway. Sparks were flying and it
slewed across the runway. There was a lot
of smoke, obviously, but it didn't burst
into flames.

Lindsey Taylor (*voice over, library pictures
of an airliner making an emergency landing
at Manchester airport in August* 1997):
Today's incident is similar to that of a
British Regional Airways ATP aircraft
which landed with one set of wheels
missing. It suffered undercarriage failure
on a flight from Ireland. But the pilot
successfully brought the plane down.
(*Dramatic pictures of plane hitting the
runway; flames coming from one of the
engines.*) The passengers were safely
evacuated. Two people were slightly
injured. In today's incident, several
passengers were taken to hospital, but
their injuries are thought to be minor.
(*Colourful, animated computer graphics
showing the layout of runways at Heathrow,
and an airliner coming in to land.*)
As the Virgin A340 came in to land, a
foam blanket had been laid across the
runway. Fire officers were standing by.
A Virgin spokesman said: (*The words are
shown in the screen.*) The aircraft
completed a normal approach and the
crew accomplished a textbook emergency
landing, and came to rest on the runway.
The emergency chutes were successfully

deployed and all the occupants left the
aircraft in an orderly fashion. (*Pictures of
crowded terminus at Heathrow.*)

Lindsey Taylor (*voice over*): Two runways
have been closed, and delays are expected
as engineers begin to investigate what
happened.

Jon Snow: Lindsey Taylor reporting there
from Heathrow. We are joined now, from
Heathrow, by Will Whitehorn, a
spokesman for Virgin Atlantic. Will
Whitehorn, let's begin with the good news.
Clearly, some excellent piloting. Nobody
was seriously hurt. Who was the pilot and
how did he do it?

Will Whitehorn (*behind him, a busy, noisy
airport scene*): Well I've just been speaking
with this pilot, Tim Barnby, who was
several years ago a UK acrobatic champion
in light aircraft, and is an ex-RAF fighter
pilot. He noticed, about an hour from
Heathrow, a warning light telling him his
left-hand undercarriage had not deployed.
He informed Heathrow tower
immediately, tried to get the undercarriage
to open, but failed, so he told the
passengers they would have to do an
emergency landing. He flew low over
Heathrow, so the ground crew could tell
him about the state of the undercarriage.
Then he landed, managing to keep the
plane upright, before he let it down on
one wing. It was a stupendous piece of
flying.

Jon Snow: That's the good news. The bad
news is the undercarriage didn't come
down properly. What does that say about
maintenance and spares?

Will Whitehorn: Well, this is a new
aircraft. We've had it about a year. The
A340 airbus has an excellent record so far

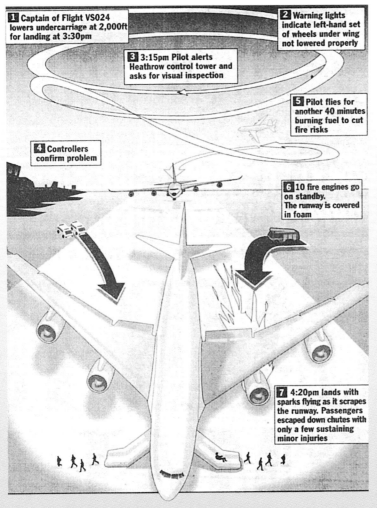

1 Captain of Flight VS024 lowers undercarriage at 2,000ft for landing at 3:30pm

2 Warning lights indicate left-hand set of wheels under wing not lowered properly

3 3:15pm Pilot alerts Heathrow control tower and asks for visual inspection

4 Controllers confirm problem

5 Pilot flies for another 40 minutes burning fuel to cut fire risks

6 10 fire engines go on standby. The runway is covered in foam

7 4:20pm lands with sparks flying as it scrapes the runway. Passengers escaped down chutes with only a few sustaining minor injuries

---

GLOSSARY

deployed – let down
disruption – upset
evacuated – got out of
maintenance – safety checks
textbook landing – perfect landing according to the rules
undercarriage – landing wheels

ACTIVITY

1 List five facts in Jon Snow's introduction to the report.
2 What action did the pilot take to reduce the risk to passengers?
3 Which eye-witness report adds most to the drama of the report? Give reasons.
4 When Will Whitehorn says, 'Well, I've just been speaking to the pilot...', what impression does this create?

---

in the years it's been in service. Obviously, the manufacturers and ourselves and the AIB are launching a full investigation.

110 **Jon Snow:** Very briefly, is it badly damaged?

Will Whitehorn: The aircraft is not that badly damaged. The landing was a textbook piece of flying so the aircraft isn't as badly damaged as it could have been.

Jon Snow: Will Whitehorn, thank you very much.

Channel 4 News, 7pm, 5 November 1997

Background

This is how the same event was reported on BBC Radio 4, 7pm News. The report was the third item in the programme, taking up 1 minute of the 5-minute broadcast.

BBC Radio Report

Pilot Tim Barnby

News reader (*live in the studio*): A Virgin Atlantic Airbus, flying from Los Angeles to London, has made an emergency landing at Heathrow airport, after one of its four
5 sets of wheels jammed in the under-carriage. The 98 passengers and 16 crew on board used emergency chutes to get out of the aircraft. At least four people were taken to hospital, but none of their
10 injuries is thought to be serious.
A Virgin spokesman, Will Whitehorn, said the captain, Tim Barnby, and his two co-pilots had used all their training and experience to bring the plane down safely.
15 **Will Whitehorn** (*taped interview*): He circled the airport for some time and used every trick in the book, as they say, to try and get that undercarriage down. Then he burned off his fuel and prepared for an emergency landing. Captain Barnby and 20 the two co-pilots who were with him did an absolutely textbook landing on the runway. They kept the aircraft upright until the last minute, then let it down gently on the wing. 25

BBC Radio 4 News, 7pm, 5 November 1997

ACTIVITY

1 What does the radio report say about the passengers who were hurt? What does the TV report say about this? Why is it sometimes difficult to report this kind of incident accurately?

2 Select two facts from the TV report which you would include in the radio report, if this had been longer. Give reasons for including them.

EXTENDED ACTIVITY

3 The person who decides how much 'air time' each report will have in a radio or TV news bulletin is the programme editor. List some things that an editor thinks about when deciding how much air time to give to a news item.

4 TV news is said to be 'picture driven'. What do you think this means? In what ways was the TV report 'picture driven'?

5 Which is the best media for reporting events like the Heathrow emergency, TV or radio? Give reasons for your answer.

6 Most of the words spoken by the news readers and reporters were scripted. The comments of the eye witnesses and the Virgin spokesman were 'off the cuff'. What are the main differences between these comments and scripted comments?

Now and then

Disaster at sea

Background

The *Titanic* sank at 2.20 am on Monday 15 April 1912, after hitting an iceberg. At first, it was thought that everyone on board was saved. This is part of a report of the sinking. The report appeared on pages 9 and 10 of *The Times* that day. There were no photographs and no eye-witness accounts.

TITANIC SUNK

TERRIBLE LOSS OF LIFE FEARED

COLLISION WITH AN ICEBERG

OFFICIAL MESSAGES

An ocean disaster, unprecedented in history, has happened in the Atlantic. The White Star liner *Titanic* on her maiden voyage, carrying nearly 2,400
5 people, has been lost near Cape Race, and according to the latest messages, there is grave reason to fear that less than 700 of the passengers and crew have been saved.
10 Early yesterday evening, the messages gave no indication of a catastrophe of such terrible magnitude, but later they became more and more serious.

STORY OF THE DISASTER

BOATS AND WRECKAGE FOUND

The White Star liner *Titanic* (46,382
15 tons), which left Southampton on Wednesday on her maiden voyage to New York, came into collision with an iceberg at a point about 41.46 North and 50.14 West off the North
20 American coast, at 10.25 on Sunday night (American time). The vessel was badly damaged and wireless messages were sent out for help. A number of other liners in her neighbourhood
25 (including the *Carpathia*, which was nearest) hastened to her assistance, but she sank yesterday morning...

HOW THE STORY UNFOLDED

New York April 15, 7.35pm
The *Titanic* sank at 2.20 this morning. No lives were lost. *Reuter*

New York April 15, 8.15pm
It was stated officially at the White 30 Star offices this evening that a number of lives had been lost in the *Titanic* disaster, but that no definite estimate could be made. *Reuter*

New York April 15, 8.20pm
The following statement was given out 35 by White Star officials: 'Captain Haddock, of the Olympic, sends a wireless message that... all the *Titanic*'s passengers and crew had been lowered safely into lifeboats.' 40 *Reuter*

New York April 15, 8.40pm
The White Star officials now admit that many lives have been lost. *Reuter*

New York April 15, 8.45pm
The following dispatch has just been received: 'The steamer *Carpathia* reached the *Titanic*'s position at 45 daybreak, but found lifeboats and wreckage only.'
The messages adds: 'All the *Titanic*'s boats are accounted for. About 675 souls have been saved of the crew and 50 passengers. The latter are nearly all women and children.' *Reuter*

The Times, Tuesday 16 April 1912

········· **ACTIVITY** ··········

1 At what time does *The Times* first hear about the sinking from the news agency *(Reuter's)* in New York?
2 How long was it before *The Times* knows the full story of the disaster?
3 List as many reasons as you can for this delay and confusion.
4 Use a dictionary to find the meaning of the following:
   a unprecedented
   b maiden voyage
   c catastrophe
   d magnitude
   e collision
   f hastened.
5 Rewrite the first section of the report ('An ocean disaster ... and more serious.') in the style of a modern newspaper or news bulletin. Devise a new headline for it.

GLOSSARY

collision – crash
indication – sign

Background

The cross-channel ferry, *Herald of Free Enterprise*, sank a mile outside Zeebrugge harbour just after 6pm on 6 March 1987. Here are some extracts from the *Guardian*'s report of the disaster.

200 feared dead as ferry capsizes

More than 200 people were feared dead early today after a British ferry bound for Dover with 543 passengers and crew on board turned over and sank outside Zeebrugge harbour.

HELICOPTERS AND small boats had saved 299 people from the wreck of the 8,000-ton *Herald of Free Enterprise*.
5 Officials said that 26 bodies had been brought ashore...

Survivors were taken from the ship by three tugs as helicopters circled overhead.
10 They moved in and plucked people from the water. Survival time in water 3°C is only a few minutes...

Two Dutch salvage tugs with
15 divers were among the first to try to rescue passengers trapped underwater. Mr John Beerman, a Dutch salvage expert, said his divers could
20 see people through portholes and door windows, surviving on trapped air. The divers later smashed their way into the vessel...

25 The report also included eye-witness reports from survivors.

Mrs Rosina Sumerfield was trapped in the ship's cafeteria for 20 minutes before divers
30 smashed through windows to put down ladders.

She said: 'It just fell on its side and the water came up

and we climbed higher to escape. It smashed all the 35 glass. There were petrol fumes because of all the cars. It was terrifying.'

Mrs Sumerfield watched while her husband, having 40 rescued their son, disappeared in the confusion.

Wayne McKenny, aged 15, from Hastings, said: 'There was lots of screaming and 45 crying after the crash.'

His father Richard, aged 65, said: 'We were very lucky the boat was so close to shore.'
The Guardian, 7 March 1987

Story in pictures

Olga Kane, a famous artist, a widow

Don Craig, works for Olga as a gardener

Molly, Olga's grandchild

ACTIVITY

1 The pictures can be arranged in different ways to tell different stories. Use Picture C as the start of a story. Use the other pictures in any order to finish the story. Write three or four sentences about each picture. Start your story like this:

Don went for a run on the beach every day. It was a bright July day. The sky was blue. The sea was calm. Don was feeling good.

Compare your story with others by your group.

2 Pick one of your own sentences and add more details. For example, you might have written a sentence like this about Picture F:

Don fell asleep holding the watch.

This could become:

Don fell asleep just after midnight. He was hot and tired. He was still holding the broken watch. He had a vivid dream …

3 Use a different order to make another story. This time start with Picture A. Use this opening:

Molly was walking on the beach with her grandmother. Every morning, rain or shine, the same walk. Every morning, the same question, "When will grandad be coming home?"

Decide how your story will end. Will it be a sad or a happy ending?

Stories with a message

The golden eagle

A man found an eagle's egg and placed it under a farmyard hen. After a few weeks, the egg hatched. The eaglet grew up with the other chickens. He clucked and cackled and scratched the earth
5   looking for worms. From time to time, just like the chickens, he flapped his wings and flew a few feet.

The years passed. One day, the eagle saw a huge bird high above the farmyard. It was
10   magnificent. It was gliding on powerful golden wings.

The eagle asked one of the chickens, "Who is that?"

"Oh, that's the king of all birds," replied the
15   chicken. "He belongs to the sky. We belong to the earth. We are just chickens."

So the eagle lived and died as a chicken, because that's what he thought he was.

Adapted from *The Song of the Bird*, by Anthony de Mello

ACTIVITY

1 Which is the best summary for The Golden Eagle? Say why.
  a Chickens should never try to become eagles.
  b Eagles are more powerful than chickens.
  c If you think like a chicken, you will remain a chicken.
  d Eagles and chickens are just the same, deep down.

2 Which is the best summary of The Indian Bird? Say why.
  a A caged bird steals the key to its cage and flies away.
  b A man is very sad when his caged bird escapes.
  c A man gives his caged bird its freedom, without knowing.
  d A clever bird tricks a cruel man.

The Indian bird

A rich man kept a bird in a cage. The bird could speak. It asked the man many times to set it free. The man always refused.

5 The man was going on a journey to India. He asked the bird if he could bring it anything back. The bird said, "Bring me back my freedom." Once again the man refused.

"Very well," said the bird, "Then go into the jungle where I used to live and tell all the other birds that I am a prisoner in this cage."

10 The man agreed to do this. He went into the jungle and spoke to the birds. As soon as he spoke, a bird fell out of a tree nearby. It lay on the ground, as if it were dead.

When the man got home the bird said, "Did you speak to the other birds?"

15 "Yes," said the man, "And one was so shocked, it fell at my feet."

As soon it heard this, the bird fell to the bottom of the cage. The man was very sad. "The news of the other bird's death has 20 killed him too," he thought. He opened the cage and took the bird out into the garden. He put it on the ground, thinking he must bury it.

Suddenly, the bird flew up into a tall 25 tree. "Now do you understand?" it said. "You put the lock on my cage. But you also gave me the key." And it flew away, free at last.

Adapted from *The Way of the Sufi*, by Idries Shah

.... **EXTENDED ACTIVITY** ....

3 The Indian Bird is trapped in a real cage. The eagle is trapped in a very different kind of cage: a cage with no bars. What is it that holds the eagle back?
Write a story about a young person who is 'trapped' like the eagle. Describe how they came to be trapped and how they escape.

Flaming Valentine

<u>14th Feb (Valentine's Day!!!)</u>

I went with a lad tonight. Still can't believe it. Keep whispering his name. Jamie. Jamie. I actually kissed a boy. It was nothing like they tell you. I don't feel ashamed. I feel special. Funny how it happened. If I hadn't missed the bus... If I hadn't been in the park... I wasn't dressed up, ready. But that's the way it is. You spend hours dressing up for a family do. Dreaming up what you're going to say to a fit cousin. And what happens? Your sister talks to him all night. Leaving you minding a baby who sicks-up on your shirt. No, it's when you're not ready. That's when it happens.

Girls my age are not supposed to be interested in lads. Especially lads like Jamie. He's a fifth year. He sits by me on the swings. Swivels round. Smiles. "Been watching you," he says. "I like you, Medina," he says. And he means it. They tell you lads are only after one thing. Even girls who go with lads say that. But Jamie's not looking at my body. He's looking into my eyes. Seeing me.

I watch his hands on the swing. Light hairs on his wrists. This cut across his thumb. I want to touch. He gets a fag out. I ask if I can light it. He smiles. I brush his creamy skin. I say, "Your poor hand." And he says, "Your poor eyes." That's all it takes. We both know then. We're off the swings and walking out of the park. He's telling me how he's wanted to talk to me, but never dared. He's asking if my parents will mind. I bite my lip. Someone will see. There'll be rows at home. But I don't care.

I went with a lad tonight. I kissed him. Snuggled against his fleece. Smelt his white lad's neck. Felt his poor hand stroking my hair. I was flying up to the stars. My poor eyes shining.

<u>15th Feb</u>

Mum found my diary. She threw a fit. Kept on and on about 'went with'.

"What do you mean, you 'went with' this boy?" I told her it just 30
meant kissing. But she didn't want to believe me. Then, when she did
believe me, she made me feel dirty.

In the end, I told her the truth, how I'd made it all up. We both cried,
then went to watch EastEnders. Later she says, "You wouldn't, would
you, Medina?" And my sister laughs and says, "Lads aren't exactly 35
queuing up for her, Mum."

<u>16th Feb</u>

Leanne Perry was snogging Jamie on the bus. I'm sick of the whole
flaming thing. Romance stinks.

Sarah Fiske

ACTIVITY

1 What does Medina's diary tell us about:
- Medina
- her mother
- her sister
- Jamie?

2 Why does Medina make up the story about kissing Jamie?

EXTENDED ACTIVITY

3 Write two short entries from a teenager's diary. The first entry should describe their fantasy – what they want to happen. The second entry should describe what really happened. You could write about one of the following:
- a disco
- a school trip
- a sporting event
- a family celebration.

Try to show the character of the diary writer through the fantasy and the way they react to the reality.

Oh yes, I knew him well ...

Background

The narrator, Thomas, is dead. He has returned, like a ghost, to his home town. He wants to find out if the people there remember him. It is very cold, and snowing hard. First, he goes into a pub.

Barmaid	Seen the film at the Elysium Mr Griffiths there's snow isn't it did you come up on your bicycle our pipes burst Monday …
Narrator	A pint of bitter, please.
Barmaid	Proper little lake in the kitchen got to wear your wellingtons when you boil an egg one and four please …
Customer	The cold gets me just here …
Barmaid	… and eightpence change that's your liver Mr Griffiths you been on the cocoa again …
Narrator	I wonder if you remember a friend of mine? He always used to come in this bar, some years ago. Every morning, about this time.
Customer	Just by here it gets me. I don't know what'd happen if I didn't wear a band …
Barmaid	What's his name?
Narrator	Young Thomas.
Barmaid	Lots of Thomases come here it's a kind of home from home for Thomases isn't it Mr Griffiths what's he look like?
Narrator	(*Slowly*) He'd be about seventeen or eighteen …
Barmaid	… I was seventeen once …
Narrator	… and above medium height. Above medium height for Wales, I mean, he's five foot six and a half. Thick blubber lips; snub nose; curly mousebrown hair; one front tooth broken

after playing a game called Cats and Dogs, in the Mermaid; speaks rather fancy; truculent; plausible; a bit of a shower-off …

In the final scene, as darkness falls, the narrator goes into the park where he used to play as a child.

GLOSSARY

truculent – bossy, aggressive
plausible – seems honest, but may not be
reservoir – lake to store water
dahlias – brightly coloured flowers

Park-keeper Oh yes, yes, I knew him well. He used to climb the reservoir railings and pelt the old swans. Run like a billygoat over the grass you should keep off of. Cut branches off trees. Carve words on the benches. Pull up moss in the rockery, go snip through the dahlias. Fight in the bandstand. Climb the elms and moon up the top like an owl. Light fires in the bushes. Play on the green bank. Oh yes, I knew him well. I think he was happy all the time. I've known him by the thousands.

Narrator We had reached the last gate. Dusk drew around us and the town. I said: What has become of him now?

Park-keeper Dead.

Narrator The Park-keeper said:

Park-keeper (*The park bell rings*) Dead … Dead … Dead … Dead …Dead … Dead.

Dylan Thomas, from the radio play *Return Journey*

ACTIVITY

1 Why do you think the barmaid's speech has few full stops? Try reading her lines as if they had commas and full stops. Then comment on the difference in your answer.
2 Describe, in your own words, Young Thomas's character. Use what was said by Old Thomas and the Park-keeper to help you.
3 Why do you think Dylan Thomas chose to end the play in the park at dusk?

EXTENDED ACTIVITY

4 Write another scene in which the narrator meets one of the following people when he leaves the pub:
   • an old school friend
   • a childhood sweetheart
   • a younger sister/brother
   • a school teacher.
   What would this person say about Young Thomas? Try to write about the positive side of his character.
5 Working in pairs, rehearse your scene. Make an audio or video recording of it.

Girl - A story from Antigua

Wash the white clothes on Monday and put them on the stone heap; wash the colour clothes on Tuesday and put them on the clothesline to dry; don't walk barehead in the hot sun; cook
5 pumpkin fritters in very hot sweet oil; soak your little clothes right after you take them off; when buying cotton to make yourself a nice blouse, be sure that it doesn't have gum on it, because that way it won't hold up well after a
10 wash; soak salt fish overnight before you cook it; is it true you sing benna in Sunday school?; always eat your food in such a way that you won't turn someone else's stomach; on Sundays try to walk like a lady and not like
15 the slut you are so bent on becoming; don't sing benna in Sunday school, you mustn't speak to wharf-rat boys, not even to give directions; don't eat fruits on the street - flies will follow you; *but I don't sing benna on Sundays at all and never in Sunday school*; this is how you
20 sew on a button; this is how you make a buttonhole for the button you have just sewed on; this is how you hem a dress when you see the hem coming down and so prevent yourself from looking like the slut I know you are so bent on becoming; this is how you iron your father's khaki
25 shirt so that it doesn't have a crease; this is how you iron your father's khaki pants so that they don't have a crease; this is how to grow okra - far from the house, because okra tree harbors red ants; when you are growing dasheen, make sure it gets plenty of water, or else it makes
30 your throat itch when you are eating it; this is how you sweep a corner; this is how you sweep a whole house, this is how you sweep a yard; this is how you smile at someone you don't like very much; this is how you smile at someone you don't like at all; this is how you smile at
35 someone you like completely; this is how you set a table for tea; this is how you set a table for dinner; this is how you set a table for dinner with an important guest; this is

44

how you set a table for lunch; this is how you set a table for breakfast; this is how to behave in the presence of men who don't know you very well, and this way they won't   40 recognize immediately the slut I have warned you against becoming; be sure you wash every day, even if it is with your own spit; don't squat down to play marbles - you are not a boy, you know; don't pick people's flowers - you might catch something; don't throw stones at blackbirds,   45 because it might not be a blackbird at all; this is how to make a bread pudding; this is how to make doukona; this is how to make pepper pot; this is how to make good medicine to throw away a child before it even becomes a

50 child; this is how to catch a fish; this is how to throw back a fish you don't like, and that way something bad won't fall on you; this is how to bully a man; this is how a man bullies you; this how to love a man, and if this doesn't work there are other ways, and if they don't work don't

55 feel too bad about giving up; this is how to spit up in the air if you feel like it, and this is how to move quickly so it doesn't fall on you; this is how to make ends meet; always squeeze bread to make sure it's fresh; *but what if the baker won't let me feel the bread?*; you mean to say that after all

60 you are really going to be the kind of woman who the baker won't let near the bread?

Jamaica Kincaid

GLOSSARY

benna – to sing a hymn in an irreverent way

dasheen – a plant grown for its edible roots

doukona – a dish made from sweet potatoes

gum – a filler to make the new cloth feel stiff, e.g. starch

khaki – green-brown colour of army uniforms

okra – an African vegetable

slut – badly brought-up girl, badly behaved

wharf-rat boys – rough boys, hooligans

ACTIVITY

1 What clues can you find in the story about the girl's age?
2 How does the mother want the girl to behave when she is a young woman? Use evidence from the story to support your answer.
3 How does the mother feel about her daughter growing up?
4 How do you think the girl feels about the advice her mother gives her?
5 Some of the things the mother talks about are trivial, like sewing on buttons. Some are serious matters, like love. Why do you think the author mixes the trivial and the serious in this way?

EXTENDED ACTIVITY

6 The daughter is alone in her room, thinking about her mother's advice. Write a monologue to show what the girl is thinking. You can use ideas from the story. You might begin like this:

> I don't want to wash whites on Monday or colours on Tuesday.
> I'll walk barehead if I want.

Try to write in the way the girl would speak. Try to include her hopes for the future, as well as some of her fears.

Thirty horse power

I remember so well walking down the platform and looking at the illuminated clock at the end which told me it was half-past eleven. I remember also my wondering whether I could get home before midnight. Then I remember the big motor, with its glaring headlights and glitter of polished brass, waiting for me outside. It was my new thirty-horse-power Robur, which had only been delivered that day. I remember also asking Perkins, my chauffeur, how she had gone, and his saying that he thought she was excellent.

"I'll try her myself," said I, and I climbed into the driver's seat …

We were just over the brow of the hill, where the grade is steepest, when the trouble began. I had been on the top speed and wanting to get her on the free; but she was stuck between gears, and I had to get her back on the top again. By this time, she was going at a great rate, so I clapped on both brakes, and then the next instant, going at fifty miles an hour, my right front wheel struck full on the right-hand pillar of my own gate. I heard the crash. I was conscious of flying through the air, and then – and then!

When I became aware of my own existence once more, I was among some brushwood in the shadow of the oaks upon the lodge side of the drive. A man was standing beside me. I imagined at first it was Perkins, but when I looked again I saw it was Stanley, a man whom I had known at college some years before, and for whom I had a really genuine affection. There was always something peculiarly sympathetic to me in Stanley's personality; and I was proud to think that I had some similar influence upon him. At the present moment, I was surprised to see him, but I was like a man in a dream, giddy and shaken and quite prepared to take things as I found them without questioning them.

"What a smash!" I said. "Good Lord, what an awful smash."

He nodded his head and even in the gloom I could see he

5

10

15

20

25

30

35

was smiling the gentle wistful smile which I connected with him.

I was quite unable to move. I had not any desire to try to move. But my senses were exceedingly alert. I saw the wreck 40
of the motor lit up by the moving lanterns. I saw the little group of people and heard the hushed voices. There was the lodge-keeper and his wife, and one or two more. They were taking no notice of me, but were very busy round the car. Then suddenly I heard a cry of pain. 45

"The weight is on him. Lift it easy," cried a voice.

"It's only my leg!" said another one, which I recognized as Perkins's. "Where's the master?" he cried.

"Here I am," I answered, but they did not seem to hear me. They were all bending over something which lay in 50
front of the car.

48

Stanley laid his hand on my shoulder, and his touch was inexpressibly soothing. I felt light and happy, in spite of all.

"No pain, of course?" he said.

55 "None," said I.

"There never is," said he.

Then a sudden wave of amazement passed over me. Stanley! Stanley! Stanley had surely died of enteric at Bloemfontein in the Boer War!

60 "Stanley!" I cried, and the words seemed to choke in my throat – "Stanley, you are dead."

He looked at me with the same old gentle, wistful smile. "So are you," he answered.

From *How It Happened*, Sir Arthur Conan Doyle

GLOSSARY

Bloemfontein – battle in the South African (Boer) war

chauffeur – person paid to drive a private car

enteric – enteric fever, typhoid fever

giddy – dazed or dizzy

grade – slope or gradient

hushed voices – low voices

inexpressibly – cannot easily be put into words

Robur – a type of early motor car

wistful – sad

ACTIVITY

1 Why does the narrator decide to drive the car?

2 What causes the accident?

3 Why does Stanley appear on the scene?

EXTENDED ACTIVITY

4 Perkins had to make a statement, telling the police what happened. Role play a conversation between him and a police officer. Remember, Perkins would be upset and confused.

5 Use the main idea from the story (a character is dead but does not know it) in a story of your own. Think about how the person dies, where they appear, and who they speak to. Use the line 'So are you' as the last line of your story.

4 Information 2 LEISURE

Hype

Claims made for games

1 HEROINE KILLS ... AND SHE'S COMING YOUR WAY.

2 BE PREPARED WE'RE ON OUR WAY!

3 Who is the deadliest of them all?

4 Sometimes you wish it was less REAL!

5 YOU DON'T RUN FROM TROUBLE, YOU RUN OVER IT.

6 the JOKE'S oN yOu iF YOU don'T geT iT.

7 INTENSE UNDERWATER ACTION Better hold your breath!

8 YOU'LL NEED ALL YOUR SKILLS TO SURVIVE.

PC magazines and leaflets

ACTIVITY

1 Which slogan(s) make you think the game:
 a has a lot of violent action
 b puts you in dangerous situations
 c has a strong female character
 d is a driving game
 e involves a submarine
 f is a humorous game
 g is a new game, due out soon
 h is so realistic it's scary?

2 Pick one of the slogans. Invent the name of a game to go with this slogan. Write 50 words about the game. Make it sound as exciting as you can.

How do they rate?

Background

Lots of computer magazines review games. Many use 5-star ratings like the one below.

★★★★★★ EXCELLENT – a perfect game. The sound and graphics are terrific. Definitely buy this game.

★★★★★ VERY GOOD – well worth the money. Very good graphics and sound. Worth buying.

★★★ GOOD – fun to play, but it has faults. Good graphics and sound, but not very original. Worth buying if you like this kind of game.

★★ AVERAGE – not a well thought-out game. Think before you buy it. Borrow it and try it first.

★ POOR – boring or too easy. Poor graphics or sound. Not worth buying.

ACTIVITY

1 In your own words, what is the main difference between a 3-star and a 4-star game?
2 List any faults that would stop a game from getting a 5-star rating.
3 In your opinion, what makes a game 'original'?

EXTENDED ACTIVITY

4 Rewrite the star ratings above to make them more appealing to teenage readers.
For example:
★★★★★ Fantastic! This game is so real, it's unreal. Play it once and you'll be playing it forever ...
5 Ask other people in your group what games they like and why. Make a list of these points. Use this list to write a description of the 'perfect game'. Try to use phrases from your rating system.

Nothing up my sleeve ...

X-ray eyes

1 You need four empty matchboxes, a long-sleeved top, a 1p coin, and a wide rubber band.

2 Secretly put the coin in one of the matchboxes. Put the matchbox on your left forearm, and hold it in place with a rubber band. Then pull down your sleeve to cover the matchbox.

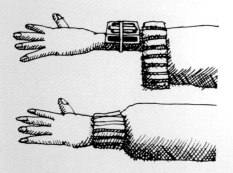

3 Place three empty matchboxes on a table.

4 Say to your friends, "There is a coin inside one of these matchboxes. Pick up a box and shake it. One of them should rattle." Your friends do this. No rattle. Tell them you have X-ray eyes and can see inside the matchboxes. Pick one with your left hand and shake it. There is a rattle!

5 Move the matchboxes around with your right hand and ask your friends to try again. Still no rattle! Pick up another matchbox with your left hand and rattle it. Xtraordinary!

From *Alan Snow's Wacky Guide to Tricks and Illusions*

ACTIVITY

1 What do you hide up your left sleeve? Would the trick work if you hid it up your right sleeve? Give reasons.

2 Would the trick work if you used three matchboxes? Give reasons for your answer.

Card trick

All you need for this trick is a pack of cards and a friend.

1 Turn the bottom card of the pack face upwards. Make sure your friend doesn't see you do this!

2 Spread out the cards, face down. Don't show the bottom card. Ask your friend to pick one card.

3 Close the pack. Turn it over.

4 Tell your friend to remember the card.

5 Ask your friend to put the card back, face down.

6 Turn your back. Spread the cards out. Your friend's card will be the only card face down.

7 Turn this card over. Hand it back to your astonished friend!

ACTIVITY

1 What equipment do you need to do this trick?
2 Why is Step 3 so important?
3 Write down two things that would make this trick go wrong.

EXTENDED ACTIVITY

With a partner
4 Find out how to do another simple trick. Write some instructions for this trick, then try it out on your group.

You're not watching that!

Background

By law, almost all videos have to be classified. It is a serious offence to sell or rent a video which has not been classified. It is an offence for a shopkeeper to sell or rent a video to someone under age.

 Universal Suitable for everyone, especially very young children.

 Universal Can be seen by all ages, nothing unsuitable for children.

 Parental Guidance Parents should check before showing to younger children. May have some violence, some sexy scenes or milder swear words.

 Not suitable for anyone under 12. May contain stronger violence and stronger swearing than a PG video.

 Not suitable for anyone younger than 15. May have a fairly adult theme. May contain scenes of sex, violence, drugs or sexual swear words unsuitable for younger teenagers.

 Unsuitable for anyone under 18. May contain strong scenes of sex and violence, as well as very explicit sexual swearing.

From *Mum, Can I Watch a Video?*, British Video Association

ACTIVITY

1 Use a dictionary to check the meanings of these words:
   • milder
   • suitable
   • brief
   • explicit.
2 In your own words, what is the difference between a PG and a U video?
3 What three things in some videos for 15 year olds might upset younger children?

EXTENDED ACTIVITY

4 How strict should parents be about what videos their children watch? Give your opinions on this. Mention the age of the children involved and various kinds of videos now available to rent or buy. Try to include information from the classifications above.

5 Role play a conversation between a parent and their 14 year old daughter/son. The teenager wants to watch a video rated 18. The parent is not very happy about this. Rehearse the conversation and make an audio or video recording of it.

Is screen violence harmful?

The question 'Is screen violence harmful?' has been the subject of much debate.

Some research shows that children who see a lot of violent images are more likely to:

- copy what they see and behave violently themselves
- think that violence is normal and acceptable
- become more timid and fearful of the world around them.

Other research shows that:

- screen violence has little effect on children

- violent behaviour in children can be caused by many things, not just one.

Even after 30 years of research, it is still not possible to prove that watching violence on the screen makes children violent. However, a Government report stated:

'There is some evidence to support the common-sense view that videos do have a bad influence on children. This may lead some vulnerable children into crime.'
(Home Affairs Committee, 1994)

From *Screen Violence - What Every Parent Should Know*, National Society for the Prevention of Cruelty to Children, 1997

ACTIVITY

1 How long has the link between screen violence and children's behaviour been studied? In your own words, what do these studies show?
2 Which sentence tells you that many different things may make a child violent?
3 Give your own views on the link between violent videos and violence in children. Support your argument with some of the information above.

EXTENDED ACTIVITY

4 Write a leaflet about video classification for young children (ages 6–11). It should answer the following questions in a clear, readable way:
- Why do we have classifications?
- What do they mean?
- Can videos affect young people?

Stomach-churning fun ...

PORT AVENTURA, SPAIN

This is the third season for Port Aventura which is partly owned by the Tussauds Group, and located near Salou, on the north-east coast of Spain. This is the park to choose if you want sun, sangria and stomach-churning fun. Rides stay open until midnight in the summer so you can stay on the beach all day and enjoy the thrills at night. New this year is the £7.5 million Stampida, a twin-track wooden racing roller coaster which joins on to a third track for junior riders. It uses more track than any other roller coaster in the world. Prepare to be subjected to a G-force roughly equivalent to a space shuttle launching. The Dragon roller coaster is always a big attraction. It reaches speeds of up to 70 miles per hour, looping the loop eight times. Make sure you follow their instructions and keep your head back. I didn't and ended up with neck ache afterwards.

The almost guaranteed sunshine and laid-back atmosphere helpcreate a party atmosphere. Although the main appeal of Port Aventura is for teenagers and thrill-seekers, it has been well thought out as the children's and adult rides are all intermingled. This enables older children to enjoy the adrenaline-pumping thrill rides while younger members of the family experience 'pink knuckle' excitement on rides such as the Waikiki mini-log ride. Do stop and watch some shows such as the Polynesian Island Dance and the Chinese acrobatics. There are no hotels on the site but plenty of accommodation in nearby Salou or elsewhere on the Costa Dorada. Alternatively, you can make it part of a city break and stay in Barcelona, which is about an hour's drive away.

Open 17 March – 26 October.
Approximately £21 for adults and £16.40 for children under 13 years old.

ACTIVITY

1 How long has Port Aventura been open?

2 In your own words, what makes the Stampida a special attraction?

3 What do the following mean:
   • stomach-churning
   • laid-back atmosphere
   • thrill-seekers
   • adrenaline-pumping
   • 'pink knuckle' excitement?

4 Give one reason why Port Aventura would appeal to:
   • a family with young children
   • a group of older teenagers.

PARC ASTERIX, FRANCE

Parc Asterix, 20 miles north of Paris, is based on the cartoon character Asterix the Gaul. Although it is only 30 minutes drive from Disneyland Paris, the
5 two parks are totally different. Parc Asterix has a very French, tongue-in-cheek sense of fun which transports you into a comic-strip world. It has a fairground-type atmosphere with plenty of performers and
10 side-shows to provide an offbeat education in the history of France. It's excellent for thrill rides. This year, there is a new £6m wooden roller coaster called Tonnerre de Zeus. White-knuckle riders should also
15 head for Goudurix, which has seven loops, guaranteed to churn the strongest guts. For a gentler introduction to roller-coaster rides, try Le Serpentin. There are also plenty of water rides, including a new one
20 this year called La Riviere d'Elis. The Great Mona Lisa Caper, which opened at Parc Asterix last year, is the largest live action show at any European theme park and includes some spectacular stunts and tricks. There are no themed hotels at Parc
25 Asterix, but plenty of reasonably priced motels to stay at nearby.

**Open 7 April – 4 September.
Approximately £16.50 for adults,
£11.50 for children 3 – 12 years, free
for under-3s.**

Both reviews from *European Theme Parks: a survival guide, Independent on Sunday,* 6 April 1997

.... **EXTENDED ACTIVITY** ....

3 A family of two adults and two children aged 5 and 15 is planning a holiday at either Parc Asterix or Port Aventura. Which do you think would be the best choice? Give reasons. Use information from the reviews to support your choice.

4 Ask other people in your group about visits they have made to theme parks. Also ask them about what kinds of attractions they expect to see in the future. Use the information you gather, and your own opinions, to prepare a short presentation on 'Theme Parks: Now and in the Future'.

.... **ACTIVITY** ....

1 What is the 'theme' of Parc Asterix? How does this make it different from Disneyland Paris?

2 Which do you think would be the best ride, the Tonnerre de Zeus or the Goudurix ? Give reasons.

Pedal power

Youngsters show that they want to cycle

Children like to cycle to school. They like the feeling of independence it gives them. A recent Sustrans survey showed that between 30 and 40 per cent want to cycle to school. But fewer than 10 per cent were able to do so. The number of aspiring cyclists is highest among 9–10 year-olds at more than 60 per cent.

Younger cyclists said the main benefit was freedom of travel.

Sixth formers were more concerned about saving money on fares.

About 20 per cent of secondary school pupils, and 30 per cent of primary pupils are driven to school. The percentages can vary greatly. At some schools with a close catchment area, up to 90 per cent of pupils cycle or walk to school. But this figure is much less when pupils have to travel long distances and cross busy main roads.

Every day, over 2 million children are driven to school, but most would prefer to cycle or walk.

Sustrans Annual Review, 1996

ACTIVITY

1 What percentage of young people would like to come to school on a bike? What percentage do cycle to school? Suggest reasons for this difference.

2 Every day, over 2 million young people are driven to school. Say how this may affect the health and safety of all school children.

What makes a Safe Route to School?

Some guidelines from the Sustrans Safe Route to School project:

✪ Routes should follow those used by most pupils at that school.

✪ Routes should be off the road, or on roads where traffic is slowed down by speed humps etcetera.

✪ Slowing down traffic is very important. Accidents involving children fall by an average of 67 per cent in 20 mph zones.

✪ Routes should be as wide as possible. Children like to travel in groups. This produces a surge at the start and end of school.

✪ Routes need to be continuous and direct. Children, like adults, don't like having to go the long way round.

✪ Secondary and older primary school children should be happy to travel on them without adults.

ACTIVITY

1 What are speed humps? What else can be used to slow down traffic on streets where children might cycle?

2 Why does slowing down traffic cut down accidents involving children?

3 In your own words, sum up the main features of a safe route to school.

Shared use paths

Many Safe Routes to School will be used by pedestrians, young and old, as well as cyclists. So cyclists must follow this code:

- ✪ Don't ride along shared paths at high speed.
- ✪ Be aware of all pedestrians.
- ✪ Always give way to pedestrians.
- ✪ Always be prepared to slow down and stop.
- ✪ Let pedestrians know you are there. Carry a bell and use it.
- ✪ Remember, some people are hard of hearing or can't see clearly. So don't assume they can see or hear you.
- ✪ Leave plenty of room as you pass. Don't try to squeeze by.
- ✪ Be very careful at blind spots such as bends.
- ✪ Use lights when it's dark.
- ✪ Where pedestrians and cyclists are divided by a white line, keep to your own side.

Sustrans Annual Review 1996

ACTIVITY

1 List some of the things cyclists might do that would cause accidents on shared paths.

2 Do you think it would be better for cyclists and pedestrians to have separate paths? Give reasons for your answer.

EXTENDED ACTIVITY

3 Write a letter to your local council about the need for safer cycle routes in your area. Use the information from Sustrans to support your argument.

Light show

Background

Blackpool illuminations:

- use more than 120 kilometres of wires and 500,000 lamps
- cost approximately £1.8 million to stage
- use £60,000 worth of electricity
- will attract more than 8 million visitors who will spend more than £200 million.

From *Facts, Figures and Fun: Blackpool Illuminations 1997*, Blackpool Tourism Department

THE GREATEST FREE SHOW ON EARTH

Back in Victorian times, Blackpool was the first town in the country to 'go electric'. A century later, the resort's love affair with light endures.

Every autumn, when other seaside towns close down, Blackpool becomes a blaze of coloured 5 lights with 'The Greatest Free Show on Earth' – Blackpool Illuminations.

Fibre optics and computer control have brought a new dimension to Britain's biggest tourist attraction. The display stretches along Blackpool's 10 famous seafront for over five miles, transforming the Promenade into a wonderland of colour.

Each year, spectacular new sections are added to the display. It's Britain's favourite autumn break, so take a trip to Blackpool Lights. 15

From *Blackpool Mini Guide*, Blackpool Tourism Department

ACTIVITY

1 How many people will come to see the lights?
2 When did Blackpool first have electric lights?
3 Which phrase tells you that Blackpool has more visitors than any other place in Britain?
4 Which phrase has the same meaning as 'a blaze of coloured lights'?

GLOSSARY

endures – lasts
resort – a town that has lots of visitors
transforming – changing

Great Expectations ...

THERE IS, OF COURSE, always a danger of disappointment when you finally encounter something you have wanted to see for a long time. But, in terms of letdown, it would be hard to exceed Blackpool's light show. I thought there would be lasers sweeping the sky, strobe lights tattooing the clouds, and other gasp-making dazzlements. Instead, there was just a rumbling process of old 5 trams decorated as rocket ships or Christmas crackers, and several miles of paltry decorations on lamp-posts. I suppose if you have never seen electricity in action, it would have been pretty breathtaking, but I'm not even sure of that. It all just seemed tacky and inadequate on rather a grand scale, like Blackpool itself. 10

What was no less amazing than the meagreness of the illuminations were the crowds of people who had come to witness the spectacle. Traffic along the front was bumper to bumper, with childish faces pressed to the windows of every creeping car. There were masses of people ambling happily along the spacious promenade. At frequent intervals, hawkers sold luminous 15 necklaces and bracelets or other short-lived diversions, and were doing a roaring trade. I read somewhere once that half of all visitors to Blackpool have been there at least ten times. Goodness know what they find in the place.

From *Notes from a Small Island*, by Bill Bryson, Black Swan, 1995

ACTIVITY

1 Which phrase tells you that the author is looking forward to seeing the lights?
2 In your own words, what does he think the lights will be like?
3 Which words best sum up how he feels about the lights?
4 Do other visitors feel the same as the author about the lights? Support your answer with quotations from the extract.

GLOSSARY

ambling – walking slowly
dazzlements – flashy attractions
encounter – meet
hawkers – street traders
meagreness – cheapness
paltry – worthless
strobe – flashing
tattooing – making a pattern on the skin
witness – see, view

EXTENDED ACTIVITY

5 How do you think people who live and work in Blackpool feel about Bill Bryson's comments? Role play a conversation between Bryson and a Blackpool resident. Use some or all of these words:
personal opinion facts fair

criticize official guidebook
visitors money tourism
6 Compare the language used in official guidebooks with more personal accounts of attractions, such as Bill Bryson's. List differences between them and say why they are different.

King Kong fact-file

A great thrill

To see a gigantic ape scaling the Empire State Building was a great thrill for cinema audiences in 1933. The magazine Picture Goers Weekly called the monster 'the mechanical marvel of this technological age'. It was released during the Depression, but grossed $25,000,000 in North America – not a bad return on an original $650,000 investment.

A strange tale

The film was based on a story by thriller writer Edgar Wallace. He died before he could start work on the script. The story is about a young actress, played by Fay Wray. She is making a film on a mysterious island. Once on Skull Island, the film crew come across a village protected by a high wall. Behind this wall lurks the Beast, called Kong. Once a year, the monster demands a human sacrifice. The villagers decide to sacrifice the young actress.

After many adventures, including being carried off by a pterodactyl, the girl is rescued. Kong is captured and taken to New York. But Kong escapes to wreak havoc on the city. He recaptures Fay Wray, with whom he has fallen in love. He makes his last dramatic stand on top of the Empire State Building. He is finally killed, gunned down by fighter planes.

Tricks of the trade

30 Nobody knew how King Kong worked. Some people said that it was a man in a gorilla suit. One magazine says that Kong is a gigantic machine, covered in bear skins and operated, from inside, by a crew of six

35 men. A full-size working model was made of King Kong's mouth and the giant hand. The main Kong was an 18in high model, and moved from the outside. The film used stop-frame photography. The animator

40 could make Kong move in a realistic way. However, this was a long and slow job. He had to change the position of the model 24 times for every second of film action.

From *Lights, Camera, Action!*, Tony Bilbow and John Gau

············ **ACTIVITY** ············

1 When was the film King Kong made, and how much did it cost?
2 Why did it create a stir when it was first shown?
3 In which two locations does most of the film's action take place?
4 In your own words, describe how the scenes involving Kong were filmed.

·········· **EXTENDED ACTIVITY** ··········

5 Write a review of the film as if you were a film-goer in 1933, seeing the film for the first time. Talk about the monster as a 'mechanical marvel' and speculate about how the film was made. Include as many details of the story as you can.

FILM FACTS

- **Big:** King Kong grows bigger in America. On the island he's 18ft high and in New York he's 24ft.
- **Noisy:** His roar is a recording of a zoo at feeding time.
- **Hairy:** His skin was made from latex rubber, and covered in cheap rabbit's hair.
- **Tough:** The mighty Kong's victims aren't even human actors – only 6in models.

The original 18" high model.

Mini-Sagas

Nemesis

They watched the old man collect his pension, followed him like twin hawks, closed on him with practised skill. Startled, the victim fell, clutching his attackers who found themselves stumbling backwards off the pavement into heavy traffic.

The coroner said, 'Accidental death'.

The old man, once a commando, knew better.

John Johns

ACTIVITY

1 What does the last line of the story tell you about the old man?
2 What do you think the title, Nemesis, means? Check, using a dictionary.

GLOSSARY

commando – soldier trained for dangerous raids
coroner – official who looks into the cause of a death

64

Home is the sailor, home from the sea

The sea was calm as they sailed for Falmouth. Steve and Carol, seasoned sailors, got into an argument within an hour. Frustrated, Carol jibed without warning and the swinging boom knocked Steve overboard. She waited two days for a storm to explain his disappearance, but his body arrived before her.

M. Rumens

GLOSSARY

boom – heavy pole that keeps the bottom of a sail stretched
jibed – turned the rudder, to change course
seasoned – experienced

ACTIVITY

1. What did Carol say to the police when she arrived at Falmouth?
2. What did the police say to Carol?
3. Use your answer to Questions 1 and 2 to make up and act out a scene between Carol and the police.

A funny thing happened on his way to the clinic to have his mole removed

As always, he scanned the crowded train, searching for his twin, separated at birth. This time was different: the faces stared back, appalled. Noticing that they glanced from him to his neighbour's paper, he read the headline, 'MURDER!' Then he looked at the photograph: his own face, minus the mole.

Caroline L. Appleby

GLOSSARY

appalled – shocked
minus – without

ACTIVITY

1. Why did the man 'scan the crowded train'?
2. Who was the murderer? Give reasons for your answer.

EXTENDED ACTIVITY

3. All three stories have the same theme. What is it and why is it a good theme for such short stories?
4. Pick one of the three mini-sagas and make it longer. Invent details such as names, times, dates and places, but keep the same ending.

Once upon a time ...

Background

The fairytale *Cinderella* is over three hundred years old. It has been translated into many languages. It has been adapted for the stage, feature films and cartoons. Here are extracts from two of the hundreds of versions of the story that exist. Both describe how Cinderella meets her Fairy Godmother.

Version A

Sadly, Cinderella went back to the kitchen and sat by the fire. All of a sudden, a log on the fire burst into flames, filling the kitchen with light. In the brightness, Cinderella noticed, for the first time, a little old lady in a cloak and
5 pointed hat – standing right next to her.

"I am your Fairy Godmother," she said kindly, "and you are going to the Ball!"

Cinderella was too surprised to speak. She had no idea she had a Fairy Godmother.

10 "Now quickly," the old lady said, "go into the garden and fetch me a pumpkin." Next, she told Cinderella to bring her the six mice and three rats that were caught in the trap near the kitchen cupboard. And last of all, she asked for six lizards from behind the garden shed.

15 With one wave of her hand the pumpkin was changed into a golden coach. The six mice turned into fine grey horses. The three rats became handsome coachmen, and lo and behold, the six lizards were smart footmen.

Version B

Cinderella sat by the fire, staring into the flames, and began to cry.

"Why are you crying?" a voice asked.

Cinderella looked up and, to her
5 amazement, saw a strange-looking woman standing next to her, watching her very seriously.

"Who are you?" she asked.

"I am your Fairy Godmother," the woman
10 replied, "and I think I can guess what is troubling you. Would you like to go to the ball too?"

"Yes. Oh yes," said Cinderella, who was so surprised that she had stopped crying
15 completely, "More than anything."

"And so you shall," said her Fairy Godmother firmly. "Go into the garden and fetch me a pumpkin."

Cinderella did as she was told, wondering
20 how a pumpkin would help her to go to the ball. Her Godmother set the pumpkin down in the courtyard and, smiling at Cinderella, began to hum under her breath. She waved her wand over the

pumpkin and suddenly it changed to a gleaming golden coach, right before 25 Cinderella's eyes.

She then watched in amazement as six mice from the mouse-trap were changed into six dapple-grey horses. There was also a big black rat in the trap. He was quickly 30 transformed into a tall coachman with a black beard.

Her Fairy Godmother even found six lizards behind the watering can, which she changed into six footmen with silk and lace 35 uniforms.

Julie Downing

ACTIVITY

1 Make a chart like this to show five things which are the same in both versions, and five things which are different.

	Version A	Version B
Cinderella is sitting by the fire	✔	✔
a log bursts into flames	✔	✘

2 Why do you think there are so many different versions of the *Cinderella* story?

3 Which version of the story do you think a four year-old would enjoy most? Give reasons for your answer.

EXTENDED ACTIVITY

4 Pick one section of Version B and rewrite it, so that it is easier for a four year-old to understand. Think carefully about the words you use and the length of your sentences. Try to give reasons for the changes you make.

"He'll be all right ... just you wait and see"

Background

The narrator, Joe, is remembering the day his father was in a car accident. Joe's mother rushes to the hospital, leaving Joe to look after his little brother, Tom. Lucy, his older sister, is at work. Joe's grandparents (his mother's parents) arrive at the house. Grandad Watson goes upstairs to play with Tom. Gran is in the kitchen with Joe.

Gran starts to twiddle the rings on her finger.

"Your dad had quite a nasty crash, Joe," she's saying. "But they're looking after him – your Mum said to tell you not to worry. I mean, doctors these days, it's amazing what they

5   can do – all those machines and things."

I don't like what I'm hearing. But Mum said not to worry. I'm just imagining things. She would have said, wouldn't she, if he had been in any real danger?

"Your Mum will ring as soon as she has any news. I'm sure

10   he'll be all right – just you wait and see."

Later, I ask, "Gran, when did Mum ring you, then?"

"Oh, about half-past two," she says much too cheerfully.

It's ten to four now and she's been looking at the clock every few minutes. The kitchen hasn't looked so clean and

15   shiny since she last visited; she even cleaned out the oven. Tom and Grandad have gone up to the park and we're sitting here in front of the TV. Don't ask me what it's about. My mind's been on other things.

I hear the police car before I see it and I'm out of the front

20   door before you can blink.

I know from the moment I see Mum's face. She doesn't have to say a word. And from the way the policewoman with her is looking at us, keeping out of the way. Mum grabs me and she's rocking me, like a baby. But I've got to

25   hear it.

"He's not dead, is he?" my voice is saying. "He's not dead, is he Mum?"

But she's not saying anything, just shaking her head, her face all screwed up and wet and ugly.

GLOSSARY

twiddle – play with, touch in an idle way

30 We've hardly got indoors when Tom's running in with Grandad behind him and he's shouting, "Hey, guess what Mum? I beat Grandad three times on Pinball!"

But he doesn't get a chance to say any more because Gran's got him by the hand and is saying in a voice that sounds like
35 she's being strangled, "Mummy's not feeling very well at the moment, Tommy..." She looks over Tom's head at Grandad and shakes her head slowly from side to side. "I bet you the tube of Smarties I've got in my handbag you couldn't beat him again."

40 "I bet I can," says Tom, running up the stairs without taking his anorak off. Grandad follows him up.

The doctor came after that and gave Mum something and she went to bed. Gran just took over and they stayed for ages. They were great; arranged for Lucy to come home,
45 and told her; did everything. But when Tom came running downstairs for his Smarties a bit later, and said, "Where's Daddy? I want to show him how I can do it," she said,

"Daddy's had to go away, darling. How about you show me?"

50 She kept saying it, too. "Don't worry about it," she'd say, each time he asked. "Mummy and Lucy and Joe are all very sad about it too, so we'll all have to try being very brave."

He stopped asking after a while. The funny thing was, at the time I was dead jealous. I'd have given anything then to
55 swap places with him, to believe that Dad had only gone away.

From *The Spying Game*, by Pat Moon, Orchard Books, 1995

········· **ACTIVITY** ·················

1 Write down some of the things Joe's grandmother says to him to try to stop him worrying.
2 Compare the way Joe and Tom behave. What does this tell you about each boy?
3 How does the author use Tom to build tension in this part of the novel?
4 Should Tom have been told the truth about his father's death? Give reasons. Compare your answers with others in the group.

·· **EXTENDED ACTIVITY** ··

5 Joe keeps a diary. Write his diary entries for the three days after the accident.
Concentrate on Joe's feelings, but also mention other members of the family. Remember, Joe says he was 'dead jealous' of his little brother. Why does he say this? Should he tell Tom the truth, if he asks? How can he help Tom and his mother?
6 Role play a conversation between Joe and his best friend at school. Joe wants to talk about what has happened, but he is not sure if his friend feels the same.

To begin at the beginning

Background

The opening of a novel is very important. A good opening makes you want to read on. It often gives you clues about the characters and the plot. It can help you to judge the 'atmosphere' of the book.

The mirror in the mist

Rain, rain all day, all evening, all night, pouring autumn rain. Out in the country, over field and fen and moorland, sweet-smelling rain, borne on the wind. Rain in London, rolling along gutters, gurgling down drains. Street lamps
5   blurred by rain. A policeman walking by in a cape, the rain gleaming silver on its shoulders. Rain bouncing off roofs and pavements, soft rain falling secretly in woodland and on dark heath. Rain on London's river, and slanting among the sheds, wharves and quays. Rain on suburban gardens,
10 dense with laurel and rhododendron. Rain from north to south and from east to west, as though it had never rained until now, and now might never stop. Rain on all the silent streets and squares, alleys and courts, gardens and churchyards and stone steps and nooks and crannies of the
15 city.
Rain. London. The back end of the year.

Susan Hill

> **GLOSSARY**
>
> **borne** – carried
> **courts** – yards
> **fen** – low-lying, marshy fields
> **heath** – flat land with low shrubs
> **laurel and rhododendron** – evergreen shrubs
> **nooks and crannies** – hidden corners
> **wharves and quays** – docks where ships are loaded

ACTIVITY

1 How does the author use the rain to create the dark, serious mood of her story?
2 How would this mood change if the rain were replaced by moonlight or snow? Rewrite part of the opening paragraph using moonlight or snow instead of rain, and comment on the difference in mood and how this might change what happens next in the novel.

1984

It was a bright cold day in April, and the clocks were striking thirteen. Winston Smith, his chin nuzzled into his breast in an effort to escape the vile wind, slipped quickly through the glass doors of Victory Mansions, though not
5 quickly enough to prevent a swirl of gritty dust from entering along with him.

The hallway smelt of boiled cabbage and old rag mats. At one end of it, a coloured poster, too large for indoor display, had been tacked on the wall. It depicted simply an
10 enormous face, more than a metre wide: the face of a man about forty-five, with a heavy black moustache and ruggedly handsome features. Winston made for the stairs. It was no use trying the lift. Even at the best of times it was seldom working, and at present the electric current was cut
15 off during daylight hours. It was part of the economy drive in preparation for Hate Week. The flat was seven flights up, and Winston, who was thirty-nine and had a varicose ulcer above his right ankle, went slowly, resting several times on the way. On each landing, opposite the lift-shaft, the poster
20 with the enormous face gazed from the wall. It was one of those pictures which are so contrived that the eyes follow you about when you move. BIG BROTHER IS WATCHING YOU, the caption beneath it ran.

George Orwell

ACTIVITY

1 Winston is the main character in the novel. What do these opening lines tell the reader about Winston?

2 What kind of mood does the author's description of the flats, Victory Mansions, create?

GLOSSARY

depicted – showed
economy drive – way of saving money
seldom – not very often
ulcer – open sore
varicose – swollen
vile – disgusting

English weather

The day was grey and cloudy, as it is sometimes in my country at the end of summer, just before the rainy period. My mother had gone with my older sister Rigbe to visit my auntie, who was going to have a baby soon. My father was
5   inside our house, sleeping, and my little brother Samuel was asleep in his arms. I was outside our house playing with my little sister Neguste on the piece of land next to our house which belongs to my father. From the east, where the sea is, there came a sudden loud roaring like thunderclaps.
10 At first, I thought it was the sound of a storm breaking I could hear. Finally the rains had arrived. I looked up into the sky to see where the thunder was coming from just at the moment fast fighter bombers dived out of the clouds and fired rockets onto the city, on to houses and shops and
15 mosques and churches, wherever they wanted to. There were some big explosions by the North gate.

As I stood watching the 'planes – I did not think to lie down – one plane flew low over our quarter and fired a rocket onto our house and the house of Mister Adam, our
20 next-door neighbour. There was a terrific explosion, and that was when my father and my brother Samuel were killed. I was thrown into the air by the blast and Neguste lost one eye. Neguste's blood was all over me. At first, I was afraid that her blood was mine, but it was God's will that I
25 was spared that day.

Neil Ferguson

The old sea dog

Background

The narrator of *Treasure Island* is a young lad called Jim
Hawkins. Jim's father owns an inn which overlooks the sea.
One day, a mysterious sailor comes to the inn.

I remember him as if it were yesterday, as he came plodding
to the inn door, his sea-chest following behind him in a
hand-barrow; a tall, strong, heavy, nut-brown man; his
tarry pigtail falling over the shoulders of his soiled blue
5   coat; his hands ragged and scarred, with black, broken
nails; and the sabre cut across one cheek, a dirty, livid
white. I remember him looking across the cove and
whistling to himself as he did so, and then breaking out in
that old sea-song that he sang so often afterwards:
10   'Fifteen men on a dead man's chest –
        Yo-ho-ho, and a bottle of rum!'
in the high tottering voice that seemed to have been tuned
and broken at the capstan bars ...

He was a very silent man by custom. All day, he hung about
15 the cove, or upon the cliffs, with a brass telescope; all
evening, he sat in a corner of the parlour next to the fire,
and drank rum and water very strong. Mostly he would not
speak when spoken to; only look up sudden and fierce, and
blow through his nose like a foghorn; and we and the
20 people who came about our house soon learned to let him
be ...

There were nights when he took a deal more rum and water
than his head would carry; and then he would sometimes
sit and sing his wicked old, wild sea-songs, minding
25 nobody; but sometimes he would call for glasses all round,
and force all the trembling company to listen to his stories
or bear a chorus of his singing. Often I would hear the
house shaking with '-ho-ho, and a bottle of rum'; all the
neighbours joining in for dear life, with the fear of death
30 upon them, and each singing louder than the other, to
avoid remark. For, in these fits, he was the most overriding
companion ever known; he would slap his hand on the
table for silence all round; he would fly up in a passion of
anger at a question, or sometimes because none was put,
35 and so he judged the company was not following his story.
Nor would he allow any one to leave the inn till he had
drunk himself sleepy and reeled off to bed.

From *Treasure Island*, Robert Louis Stevenson

GLOSSARY

bear a chorus – join in
by custom – usually
capstan – machine used to raise the anchor on a ship
cove – sheltered bay
livid – bluish-grey
overriding – forceful
parlour – sitting room
plodding – walking slowly
reeled – swayed
sabre – sword
soiled – dirty
tottering – shaky

ACTIVITY

1 The author describes in detail the appearance of the old sailor. Pick one or two of these physical details and say how each offers a clue to the man's character.

2 We learn most about the old sailor's character through the effect he has on Jim and the others at the inn. Use this evidence, as well as clues from his appearance (see Question 1) to write a pen portrait of the old sailor.

EXTENDED ACTIVITY

3 Write a conversation between Jim and the old sailor. Jim would like to hear about all the strange, faraway places the sailor has been to. He is also rather afraid of the man. Try to show this tension in the conversation. Try to match the way the sailor speaks and what he talks about with your answer to Question 2.

Getting a life

I was on my way to work, stuck in the usual traffic, listening to the radio, when I glanced out of the window and suddenly saw my life going the other way, sitting on the back of a lorry.

5   I recognized it immediately – even though I still hadn't lived most of it – it was definitely my life, and it was heading out of town, against the grain of the morning rush hour. It's not the kind of life you can easily mistake. I'd been planning it for years. I knew it was mine from the
10 shape of it, the wealth of opportunities in it, from that twinkle in its eye. It was my life. No doubt about it.

My blood ran cold. I was gripped by panic. "My life," I thought, "It's been stolen by unscrupulous thieves. They've hijacked it. They'll probably respray it now, and sell it
15 abroad to some rich, bored nobody, who's wanted an interesting life for years."

Not, I hasten to add, that my life was interesting. At least, not at that time. On the contrary, it was very dull and routine. But the life ahead of me – my new life as an
20 international traveller, a world-renowned wit and raconteur, as a film star, best-selling novelist, philanthropist, lover of beautiful women and family man – it was a good one. And now it was fading from sight in my rear view mirror.

25 I couldn't just let it disappear like that. Not simply to get into the office on time. I could be late for one day. This was important. A life was at stake – mine.

I did a U-turn in the road and gave chase. After a few minutes, I caught up with it. For a second, I thought that
30 maybe they'd been trying to deliver it, and having found me not at home, were taking it back to the depot. But then I realised what a foolish thought this was. It had been stolen. No doubt about that.

A few minutes later, we were on the motorway. My old
35 car isn't in the best of health – not like the Ferrari I was due to have in the new life ahead – and I had trouble keeping up with the truck. Suddenly, my car lost speed and steam came from under the bonnet. I had to pull over on to the hard shoulder and find a telephone.

40 That was the last I saw of the lorry and my wonderful life: the two of them vanished over the horizon together, on their way to who-knew-where.

I felt like crying. My beautiful life, gone forever. I'd never get another one like it. I'd been dreaming of it for
45 years, and I hadn't even remembered to take the lorry's number. Yes, I felt so bad I could have cried.

The patrolman arrived and got me back on the road. But it was hopeless trying to catch the lorry, so I drove back into town and headed for the police station. On my way, I
50 stopped to phone Miss Peasley at the office.

"It's me, Miss Peasley," I said. "I'm sorry I'm going to be late, my life's been stolen. I saw it this morning on the back of a lorry."

"Life?" she said. "What life, Plumcott? I wasn't aware
55 that you had a life. Not to speak of. You've got your nine to five here, and your bicycle outings at the weekend, and that's about it, isn't it?"

"Yes, Miss Peasley," I conceded. "It may seem that way, although you shouldn't judge a man by his anorak. But I mean my other life. You know. The life I should have had as a film star and an international sportsman. It was obviously on its way to me but it's been abducted. It might take me a while to get things sorted out. I'm just on my way to the police station to report the theft. I should be into the office by mid-morning at the latest."

I hung up the phone and hurried off to the police station.

"Good morning, Sergeant," I said. "I wish to report a theft, as a matter of some urgency."

He reached for a report sheet.

"Oh yes, sir," he said. "And what property have you lost?"

"Had stolen," I reminded him. "Someone has stolen my life. I saw it this morning on a lorry. I tried to give chase but I lost it on the motorway."

"Your life, you say, sir? Someone's stolen your life? Are you sure you're not making this up, sir?"

"I know it sounds far-fetched," I said. "But it's true. A whole life. It's been taken from under my nose."

"You'd better give us a full description then, sir, if you would. Now, this life of yours ... what exactly did it look like?"

From *Getting a Life*, a story for radio by Alex Shearer

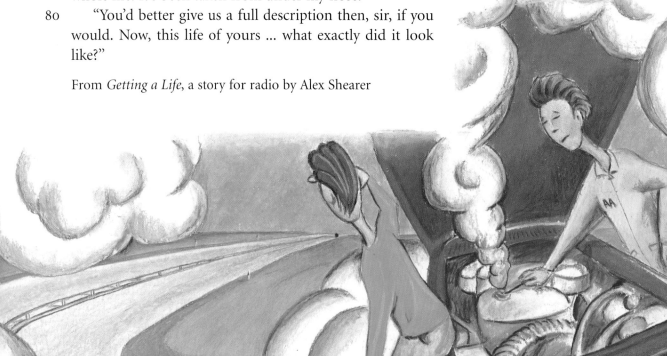

ACTIVITY

1 What does the first paragraph tell you about the kind of story 'Getting a Life' is?
2 What clues does the extract give about the character of the narrator, Mr Plumcott?
3 In your own words, describe the life that Mr Plumcott sees ahead of him. How does this future life compare with his present one?
4 The story was written especially for radio. What kinds of things does an author have to think about when writing a story for a radio audience? Can you identify any of these in the extract?

EXTENDED ACTIVITY

5 Later in the story, the police contact Mr Plumcott and ask him to go to their lost property department. Describe Mr Plumcott's visit. What sort of 'lost property' does he see there? Remember, the opening suggests the story is a fantasy – so anything might happen! Does he find his missing life? Or someone else's perhaps?
Look back at your answer to Question 2. Remember, you are writing for radio.
6 Make up and rehearse a short conversation between you and a friend, which starts with the following opening line:
I was on my way to school one morning when I saw my life going down the road on the back of a lorry.

MAZE MAZE MAZE MAZE
MAZE MAZE MAZE
MAZE
MAZE MAZE MAZE MAZE
MAZE MAZE MAZE MAZE
MAZE MAZE MAZE
MAZE MAZE
MAZE MAZE MAZE MAZE MAZE

apple apple

wormworm

waveswaveswaveswaveswaveswaveswaveswaves
waveswaveswaveswaveswaveswaveswaves
sssssssss

ROCK
ROCKROCK
ROCKROCKROCK
ROCKROCKROCK

The Eraser Poem

The eraser poem.
The eraser poem
The eraser poe
The eraser po
The eraser p
The eraser
The erase
The eras
The era
The er
The e
The
Th
T

Louis Phillips

Kite

I'm part of a project on flight I'm supposed to attain a great height. But unfortunately I got stuck in a tree so it looks like I'm here for the night

June Crebbin

Miniskirt

miniskirtminiskirt
miniskirtminiskirtmi
niskirtminiskirtminisk
irtminiskirtminiskirtmin

legleglegleglegleglegleglegleglegleg   legleglegleglegleglegleglegleglegleg

shoe   shoe

Anthony Mundy

Dodo

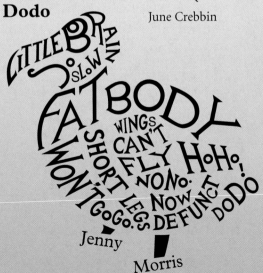

Jenny
Morris

Bananas

The Uncertainty of the Poet

I am a poet.
I am very fond of bananas.

I am bananas.
I am very fond of a poet.

I am a poet of bananas.
I am very fond.

A fond poet of 'I am, I am' –
Very bananas.

Fond of 'Am I bananas?
Am I?'– a very poet.

Bananas of a poet!
Am I fond? Am I very?

Poet bananas? I am.
I am fond of a 'very'.

I am of very fond bananas.
Am I a poet?

Wendy Cope

82

ACTIVITY

1 Which of the following sentences best sums up the poem? Give reasons. This poem is:

a a warning not to eat too many bananas

b all about the strange thoughts you have if you eat bananas

c about the fun you can have with words like 'bananas'

d about a very strange woman who likes bananas.

2 The poet shuffles the words of the first verse, like a card player shuffling a pack of cards. This is how she creates her poem. Try shuffling these two sentences, and see if you can make a poem:

> The orange rolled off the table.
> The cat ate it.

You might start like this:

> The cat rolled off the table.
> The orange ate it!

Ears like bombs, teeth like splinters

A

Ears like bombs, teeth like splinters:
a blitz of a boy was Timothy Winters.
Charles Causley

B

The sea is a hungry dog, giant and grey.
He rolls on the beach all day.
James Reeves

C

The yellow sun was ugly,
like a raw egg upon a plate.
Elizabeth Bishop

D

As I walked out one evening,
Walking down Bristol Street,
The crowds upon the pavement
Were like fields of harvest wheat.
WH Auden

E

When you see me sitting quietly,
like a sack left on the shelf ...
Maya Angelou

F

The wind was a torrent of darkness among the
*   gusty trees,*
The moon was a ghostly galleon tossed upon
*   cloudy seas.*
Alfred Noyes

G

Said the Wind to the Moon, "I will blow you out.
You stare, in the air, like a ghost in a chair.
Always looking what I am about ... "
George Macdonald

H

In the bleak midwinter, frosty wind made moan.
Earth stood hard as iron, water like a stone.

Christina Rossetti

I

Dead, the word like a stone in his throat.

Graham Mort

J

Anger lay by me all night.
His breath was hot upon my brow.

Elizabeth Daryush

GLOSSARY

blitz – an attack by bombers
brow – forehead
galleon – sailing ship
torrent – fast flowing river

ACTIVITY

1 Complete this table. The first one has
been done for you.

Quotation	What is being compared?
A Timothy's ears	bombs
Timothy's teeth	splinters
the boy, Timothy	a blitz
B	

2 Look again at Quotations F and G.
Which one paints the most vivid
picture? Give reasons for your answer.

3 Pick another quotation and say in your
own words what kind of picture the
poet was trying to create.

EXTENDED ACTIVITY

4 Imagine a person who is very shy and
doesn't say very much. Think of as
many comparisons as you can to
describe that person. You could say:
S/He was very quiet.
Or
S/He was as quiet as an ant.
Or
S/He was as quiet as an ant in carpet
slippers.
Now think of ways of describing a
bossy person:
S/He was as bossy as ...
Put the two comparisons together
in a short poem which describes
what happens when the two people
meet. Think of a title which fits the
mood of the poem. Prepare a
rehearsed reading of the poem. With
a partner, work out a dramatic way to
read it.

Ways of looking, ways of seeing ...

'*Two men look out through the same bars;*
One sees mud – and one sees stars'

Frederick Langbridge

Background

Poets often look at everyday objects or events with fresh eyes. In this poem, Rachel Field sees skyscrapers as tired, longing to lie down and sleep ...

Skyscrapers

Do skyscrapers ever grow tired
of holding themselves up high?
Do they ever shiver on frosty nights
with their tops against the sky?
Do they feel lonely sometimes,
because they have grown so tall?
Do they ever wish they could just lie down
and never get up at all?

Rachel Field

ACTIVITY

1 If skyscrapers could speak, what would they say? Write a short monologue which includes the following words:
- sleep
- tired
- hot-water bottle
- bedtime story
- bed

Make sure your monologue has the same fantasy quality as the poem.

2 Prepare a rehearsed reading of your monologue.

Background

People usually go to an auction to buy second-hand furniture, but in this poem, the moon is for sale ...

Auctioneer

Now I go down here and bring up a moon.
How much am I bid for the moon?
You see it a bright moon and brand-new.
What can I get to start it? how much?
What! who ever heard of such a bid for a moon?
Come now, gentlemen, come.
This is a solid guaranteed moon.
You may never have another chance
to make a bid on such a compact
eighteen-carat durable gold moon.
You could shape a thousand wedding rings
out of this moongold.
I can guarantee the gold and the weddings
will last forever
and then a thousand years more.
Come gentlemen, no nonsense, make me a bid.

Carl Sandburg

GLOSSARY

auction – sale where goods go to the highest bid
auctioneer – person who runs an auction
compact – small, neat
durable – long-lasting
eighteen-carat gold – almost pure gold
guarantee – promise

ACTIVITY

1 Practise reading the poem as if the auctioneer was speaking it.
2 Write a poem about the same auctioneer trying to sell one of the following:
   • the Atlantic Ocean
   • your school
   • your favourite pop group or football team.

EXTENDED ACTIVITY

3 Write about an ordinary object in the fanciful way the poet writes about the skyscrapers. You can write a poem (with or without rhymes) or monologue.
For example: You could write about a vacuum cleaner as if it were a living thing, and the dust it collects are its memories.
Next, try to write about another object or situation in a more serious way. Here are some possible starting points:
a burning leaves and garden rubbish; watching the smoke turn into words ...
b using a washing machine; the tumbling laundry becomes faces, the rumble of the machine sounds like distant voices ...
c putting new wallpaper on your bedroom, peeling off the old paper; peeling away memories, emotions, dreams ...

Growing pains

How to Talk

It was on a ferris wheel
I was introduced to
the art of conversation.
She was thirteen,
I was fourteen;
many times we passed the point
where we climbed on.
How high it is, up here, she said
when we were near the top.
I could see my name
on the tip of her tongue.

Andrew Johnson

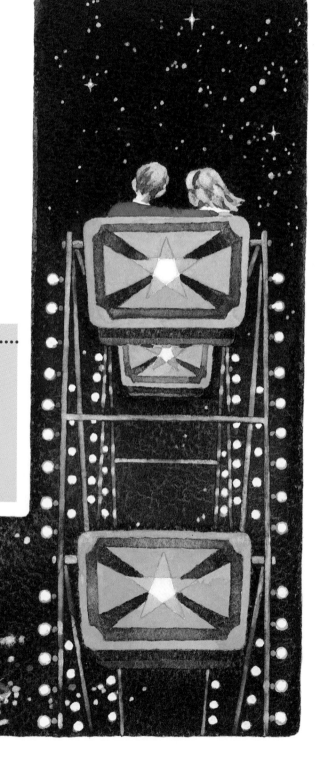

.... **ACTIVITY** ....

1 Why is the image of the big wheel turning and turning a good one to use in this particular poem?
2 Why does the boy say he could see his name on the tip of the girl's tongue? How does this link with the title of the poem?

First Frost

In the telephone booth a girl
is turning into ice.
Huddled in a thin coat
her face is tear-stained
and smeared with lipstick.
She wears earrings made out of glass
and breathes on fingers that freeze.
She will have to go home now.
Alone along the icy street.
First frost. A beginning of losses.
The first frost of telephone phrases.
Winter glistens on her cheek.
The first frost of having been hurt.

Andrei Voznesensky

If I Might Be an Ox

If I might be an ox,
An ox, a beautiful ox,
Beautiful but stubborn:
The merchant would buy me,
Would buy me and slaughter me,
Would spread my skin,
Would bring me to the market,
The coarse woman would bargain for me,
The beautiful girl would buy me.
She would crush perfumes for me,
I would spend the night rolled up round her,
I would spend the afternoon rolled up round her.
Her husband would say: 'It is a dead skin.'
But I would have her love.

Anon: a love song from the Galla tribe in Ethiopia

GLOSSARY

merchant – trader, shopkeeper
slaughter – kill

Seven Wishes

Why can't I be the band that binds your
forehead, so close to your thoughts?
Why can't I be the nub of sweetcorn
you shred with your wildcat's teeth?
Why can't I be the thread of many colours
that slides through your fingers on the loom?
Why can't I be the sand in your moccasins
that dares to stroke your toes?
Why can't I be your night's dreams
when you moan in the black arms of sleep?

Anon: Pueblo Indian

from: As I Walked Out One Evening

I'll love you dear, I'll love you
Till China and Africa meet
And the river jumps over the mountain
And the salmon sings in the street.

I'll love you till the ocean
Is folded and hung up to dry
And the seven stars go squawking
Like geese about in the sky.

WH Auden

GLOSSARY

moccasins – soft leather shoes
nub – small piece

ACTIVITY

1 The poet repeats the
  phrase 'Why can't I...'
  five times. How does
  this affect the mood the
  poem creates?
2 Add three more 'wishes',
  using these words or
  some of your own:
  • sun   • day   • stars
  • forest • moon • fire
  • rain • night • river

ACTIVITY

1 What does the image of China and
  Africa meeting tell us about how
  strongly the poet feels?
2 Pick another image from the poem and
  say how this also shows the strength of
  the poet's love.

Love without Hope

Love without hope, as when the young bird-catcher
Swept off his tall hat to the Squire's own daughter,
So let the imprisoned larks escape and fly
Singing about her head as she rode by.

Robert Graves

.... **ACTIVITY** ....

1 What kind of mood is the poet trying to create with the image of the birds escaping from the young man's hat?
2 Why does the young man 'love without hope'?

.... **EXTENDED ACTIVITY** ....

3 Which of the poems has the most to say to a young person about love? Give reasons.
4 Why do you think there are so many poems written about love? Read some more love poetry. Find a poem you like and say why you like it.
Compare it with one of the love poems here.

Storylines

Lochinvar

O, young Lochinvar is come out of the west,
Through all the wide Borders his steed is the best;
And save his good broadsword he weapons had none,
He rode all unarmed and he rode all alone.
5   So faithful in love, and so dauntless in war,
There never was a knight like the young Lochinvar.

He stayed not for brake, and he stopped not for stone,
He swam the Esk river where ford there was none;
But ere he alighted at Netherby gate
10   The bride had consented, the gallant came late:
For a laggard in love, and a dastard in war,
Was to wed the fair Ellen of brave Lochinvar.

So boldly he entered the Netherby Hall,
Amongst bridesmen, and kinsmen, and brothers and all:
15   Then spoke the bride's father his hand on his sword
(For the poor craven bridegroom said never a word)
"O come ye in peace here, or come ye in war,
Or to dance at our bridal, young Lord Lochinvar?"

"I long wooed your daughter, my suit you denied –
20   Love swells like the Solway, but ebbs like its tide –
And now am I come, with this lost love of mine,
To lead but one measure, drink one cup of wine.
There are maidens in Scotland more lovely by far,
That would gladly be bride to the young Lochinvar."

25   The bride kissed the goblet: the knight took it up,
He quaffed down the wine, and he threw down the cup.
She looked down to blush, and she looked up to sigh,
With a smile on her lips, and a tear in her eye.
He took her soft hand, ere her mother could bar –
30   "Now tread we a measure!" said young Lochinvar.

GLOSSARY
bar – stop
brake – a clump of bushes or trees
consented – agreed
craven – cowardly
dastard – a coward
dauntless – brave
denied – stopped, refused
ebbs – flows out
ere – before
ford – shallow crossing place in a river
gallant – knight
goblet – glass for drinking wine
kinsmen – family
laggard – someone who lags behind
measure – dance
quaffed – drank quickly
steed – a fast horse
suit – an offer or wish of marriage
tread – dance
wooed – loved

92

So stately his form, so lovely her face,
That never a hall such a galliard did grace;
While her mother did fret, and her father did fume,
And the bridegroom stood dangling his bonnet and plume;
35 And the brides-maidens whispered, "Twere better by far,
To have matched our fair cousin with young Lochinvar."

One touch of her hand, one word in her ear,
When they reached the hall door, and the charger stood near;
So light to the croupe the fair lady he swung,
40 So light to the saddle before her he sprung!
"She is won! we are gone, over bank, bush, and scaur;
They'll have fleet steeds that follow," quoth young Lochinvar.

There was mounting 'mong Graemes of the Netherby clan;
Forsters, Fenwicks, and Musgraves, they rode and they ran:
45 But the lost bride of Netherby ne'er did they see.
So daring in love, so dauntless in war,
Have ye e'er heard of gallant like young Lochinvar?

Sir Walter Scot

GLOSSARY	
charger	– swift horse
croupe	– the back end of a saddle
fleet	– fast
fret	– worry
fume	– be very angry
galliard	– a kind of dance
ne'er	– never
scaur	– rocky slope, cliff
'twere	– it would be

●●●●●●●●●●●●●●●●●●●●●●●●●●●● **ACTIVITY** ●●●●●●●●●●●●●●●●●●●●●●●●●●●●

1 Why does Lochinvar go to Netherby Hall?

2 Using evidence from the poem, say how the following feel when Lochinvar arrives after the wedding:
  • Ellen's mother
  • Ellen's father
  • the bridegroom
  • the brides-maidens.

3 What does the verse beginning 'The bride kissed the goblet ...' tell us about Ellen's feelings towards Lochinvar?

4 Prepare a rehearsed reading of the poem. Share the reading. Try to use contrasting voices to highlight the drama of the story.
Role play a conversation between two characters in the poem.

5 Retell the story in your own words, but in a modern setting. Your opening line might be about Lochinvar arriving at the church on a high-powered motorbike. Rehearse your story and make an audio or video recording of it.

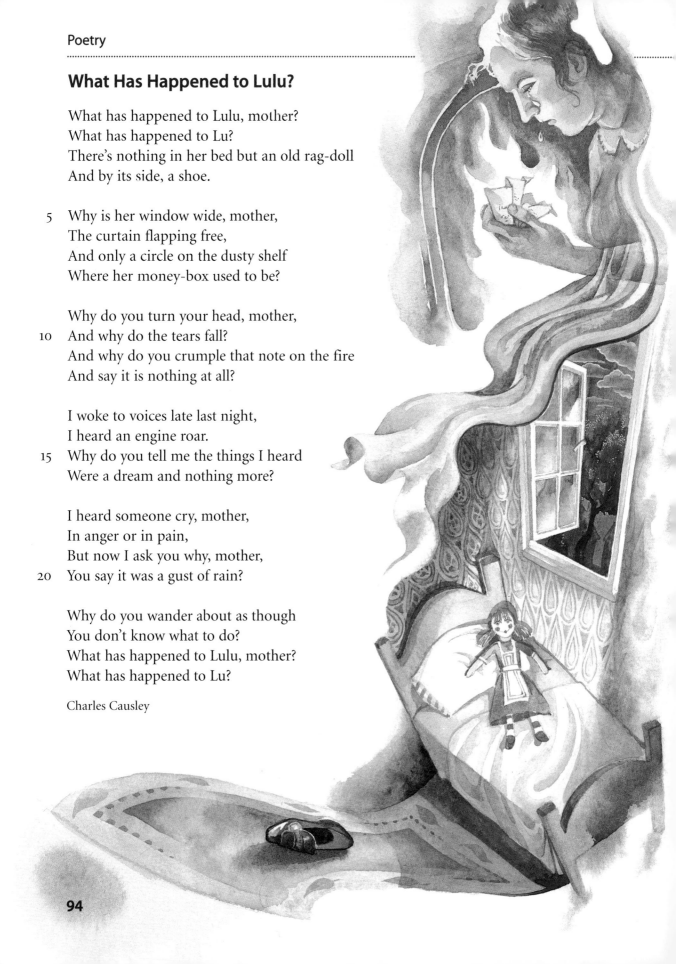

What Has Happened to Lulu?

What has happened to Lulu, mother?
What has happened to Lu?
There's nothing in her bed but an old rag-doll
And by its side, a shoe.

5   Why is her window wide, mother,
The curtain flapping free,
And only a circle on the dusty shelf
Where her money-box used to be?

Why do you turn your head, mother,
10 And why do the tears fall?
And why do you crumple that note on the fire
And say it is nothing at all?

I woke to voices late last night,
I heard an engine roar.
15 Why do you tell me the things I heard
Were a dream and nothing more?

I heard someone cry, mother,
In anger or in pain,
But now I ask you why, mother,
20 You say it was a gust of rain?

Why do you wander about as though
You don't know what to do?
What has happened to Lulu, mother?
What has happened to Lu?

Charles Causley

ACTIVITY

1 What does the poem tell us about Lulu and how the narrator feels about her?
2 What kind of mood does the poet want to create with the image of 'the curtain flapping free'?
   Pick two more Images from the poem which create the same mood.
3 In your own words, say what you think happened to Lulu and why.

EXTENDED ACTIVITY

4 Write a poem about Lulu that answers some of the questions in the original. Write two or three four-line verses. Use rhymes if you can.
5 Comment on the way both Causley and Scot use rhymes and images to create a mood and tell their story.
   Say which poem you like best and why. Support your answer with quotations from both poems.

Get noticed

Slogans

Background

You work for an advertising agency called Get Noticed.
Part of your job is thinking up slogans like the ones below:

3 TYPHOO PUT THE T IN BRITAIN

1 COUGHS AND SNEEZES SPREAD DISEASES

4 We are not alone

5 Fly the flag

2 Put a tiger in your tank

6 Fresh to the last slice

ACTIVITY

1 Match the slogans above with these products:
  a tea bags
  b a flu medicine
  c bread
  d an airline
  e petrol
  f TV series on UFOs.

2 Think up another slogan for three of the products.

3 Some slogans use puns (wordplay) to give them more than one meaning. Identify the word(s) which give these slogans their double meanings:
  a We've got lots of bright ideas (DIY lighting dept)
  b Look into the future (television sets)
  c Are you on the ball? (video football game)
  d Sweet Dreams (chocolate bar)
  e Impressing your guests is a piece of cake (chocolate cake).

4 Pick one of the slogans that you like from Questions 1 and 3, and say why you think it is good.

Types of type

Background

Lettering comes in hundreds of different shapes and sizes. When you design an advert, it is important to pick the right lettering. It must match the product and the 'mood' of the advert.

Where to advertise?

Background

Part of your work at Get Noticed (the advertising agency) is making sure the adverts are placed in the right magazines and newspapers, so they reach the right target audience. Here is some information about the readership of four magazines:

Magazine	15-34 yrs	35-54 yrs	55+ yrs	Female	Male
A	32%	31%	37%	52%	48%
B	73%	9%	8%	73%	27%
C	37%	46%	17%	8%	92%
D	9%	21%	70%	62%	38%

ACTIVITY

1 Which of the four magazines is read mainly by young women?
2 What can you tell about the readership of the other three magazines?
3 Which magazine might be a fishing magazine, such as *Fishing Monthly*? Give reasons.

EXTENDED ACTIVITY

4 In which of the four magazines would you place adverts for the following:
• family holidays
• pet food
• computers
• make-up?
Give reasons, using the phrase 'target audience'.

Reaching a wider audience

Background

Get Noticed gives advice on advertising on TV, as well as in newspapers and magazines. The figures below and top right show the cost of adverts.

NRS, 1997

Costs of full-page, colour advert in newspapers		
Sunday national newspaper	£30,000	1,500,000 readers
Daily national newspaper	£20,000	1,000,000 readers
Weekly local newspaper	£2,000	20,000 readers

Costs of advertising on national TV			
National TV	**10 sec advert**	**30 sec advert**	**60 sec advert**
Before 5 pm	£5,000	£9,000	£15,000
Between 5 pm and 8 pm	£15,000	£25,000	£50,000
Between 8 pm and 11 pm	£30,000	£50,000	£100,000

Laser/Granada TV 1997

ACTIVITY

1 How much would the following adverts cost:
  • a 30 second advert on national TV at 10.30 pm
  • a 60 second advert on national TV at 5.30 pm
  • a full-page colour advert in *The News of the World*?

2 A company selling Christmas crackers had £30,000 to spend on advertising. Suggest two ways it could spend this money. Say which you think would be best. Give reasons.

3 In what ways are TV adverts different from newspaper adverts?

4 Is it easier to 'target' an audience with TV or newspaper adverts? Give reasons.

5 Think of one product that would be better to advertise on TV, rather than in newspapers. Give reasons.

TeenScene

124 Angel Street
Newcastle-upon-Tyne
NE17 6JS

Dear Get Noticed,

Teen Scene are looking for an advertising agency to help us to promote our new range of activity holidays for 12-14 year olds. We will offer the usual activities such as climbing, riding, and mountain biking. But this year, youngsters will also be able to make pop music videos, surf the net, and play virtual reality games in our new £5 million Techno-Challenge Dome. We would be very interested to hear how Get Noticed can help us to get noticed. Please let us have your ideas as soon as possible and we will set up a meeting.

Yours sincerely,

Lee Holmes

Lee Holmes

EXTENDED ACTIVITY

6 Write a reply to Teen Scene. Set it out as a business letter. Use the information above to give them a clear idea of when and where to advertise.
You might also mention costs, the target audience and possible slogans.

Legal, decent, honest and truthful

The work of the ASA

▶ ASA stands for Advertising Standards Authority. The ASA makes sure that non-broadcast adverts are 'legal, decent, honest and truthful'.

▶ The ASA has a Code – a set of rules written by the advertising industry. If an advert breaks these rules, then it may have to be withdrawn.

How does the Code affect young people?

The Code affects young people in many ways. For example:

▶ Adverts for alcohol: These must not be aimed at young people under 18. They must not say drinking will make you sexy or good at sports.

▶ Cigarette adverts: Anyone shown smoking must look over 25. Smoking must not be linked to romance or sex. New laws might soon prevent all cigarette advertising.

▶ Adverts aimed at children and children in adverts: Adverts must not cause children to be harmed physically or emotionally. They must not make children feel inferior or unpopular.

How many people complain?

This graph shows the number of complaints between 1980 and 1996.

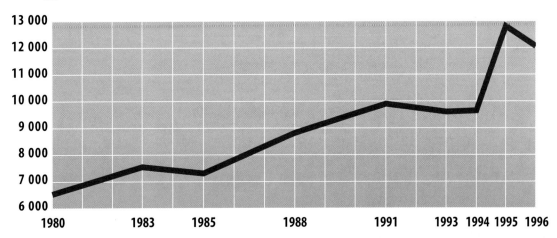

In 1996, there were over 12,000 complaints, about 8,409 adverts. Very few adverts actually broke the ASA's rules. The ASA asked that 720 should be withdrawn.

What do people complain about?

In 1996, most complaints were about leisure, clothes, motoring, and health and beauty products. Nearly 850 complaints were about the sexist way women were shown in adverts.

Advertising Standards Authority, 1997

ACTIVITY

1 Use a dictionary to find the meaning of:
   • legal
   • inferior
   • withdrawn
   • portrayed
   • sexist.
2 Why does the ASA have such strict rules about cigarette and alcohol adverts? What other types of adverts would you expect the ASA to keep a close eye on? Give reasons.
3 When is an advert 'dishonest' ?
4 What does the graph show? What does this tell you about the work of the ASA?

EXTENDED ACTIVITY

5 Write a toy advert which breaks the ASA rules on children. State clearly how your advert breaks the ASA rules. Then rewrite the advert, putting it right.

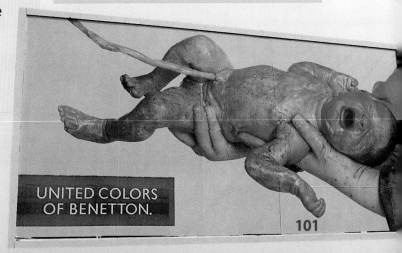

UNITED COLORS OF BENETTON.

101

Adverts in the dock

Background

Every month, the ASA publishes a report about the
complaints it receives. This is how the report is set out:

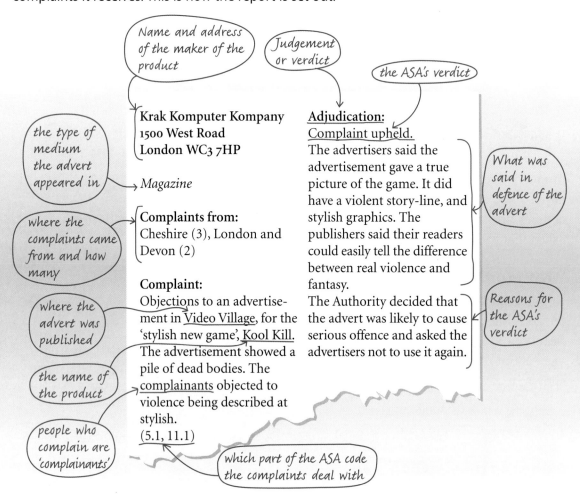

Name and address of the maker of the product

Judgement or verdict

the ASA's verdict

the type of medium the advert appeared in

where the complaints came from and how many

where the advert was published

the name of the product

people who complain are 'complainants'

What was said in defence of the advert

Reasons for the ASA's verdict

which part of the ASA code the complaints deal with

Krak Komputer Kompany
1500 West Road
London WC3 7HP

Magazine

Complaints from:
Cheshire (3), London and
Devon (2)

Complaint:
Objections to an advertisement in Video Village, for the
'stylish new game', Kool Kill.
The advertisement showed a
pile of dead bodies. The
complainants objected to
violence being described at
stylish.
(5.1, 11.1)

Adjudication:
Complaint upheld.
The advertisers said the
advertisement gave a true
picture of the game. It did
have a violent story-line, and
stylish graphics. The
publishers said their readers
could easily tell the difference
between real violence and
fantasy.
The Authority decided that
the advert was likely to cause
serious offence and asked the
advertisers not to use it again.

ACTIVITY

1 In which magazine did the advert appear?
2 How many people complained about the advert?
3 In your own words, why did they complain?

4 How did the advertisers and publishers try to defend the advert?
5 If this had been a real complaint, would you have agreed with the ASA's decision? Give reasons for your answer.

Jeans scene

In 1997, the ASA received complaints about two poster adverts for jeans.

One poster featured a picture of a woman's leg. She was wearing jeans and a stiletto-heeled boot. Her toe was resting on the naked buttocks of a man, who was lying at her feet. The slogan was 'Put the boot in'. Seventy-seven people complained to the ASA. They said the advert was offensive and encouraged violence.

The other advert showed a shooting target in the shape of a man. This target was full of bullet holes. The headline said 'Body piercing while-u-wait'.

One person complained about this advert. They said it was threatening and encouraged violence.

ASA, 1997

ACTIVITY

1 Why did people complain about the adverts?

2 Do you think the ASA upheld the complaints? Give reasons for your answers.

3 Role play a conversation between the writer who made up one of the jeans adverts and a person who complained to the ASA about the advert.

EXTENDED ACTIVITY

4 Adverts aimed at young people often use very eye-catching images. Some of these images are designed to shock. Sometimes they offend older readers/viewers. Make a collection of adverts aimed at teenagers. Do the same for adverts aimed at older people. Write about the difference between the two. Talk about how colour, lettering, visual images and words are used in both, and the impressions these create. Show clearly what makes an advert appeal to a particular audience. For example, what kind of advert might persuade young people, but not older people?

A global media event

What will they do without her?

"YOU SEE YOURSELF as a good product that sits
on a shelf and sells well, and people make a lot of
money out of you," Diana, the Princess of Wales,
said bluntly in the controversial Panorama
5 interview.

Recent pictures of the princess with her
friend Dodi Fayed were thought to have sold at
least 750,000 extra newspapers, according to
latest figures.

10 Magazines with a picture of Diana on the
front could see a circulation leap of as much as
30–40 per cent.

The book industry also benefited from the
princess. Andrew Morton's book, *Diana: Her True
15 Story*, published in 1992, revealed details of the
princess's struggle with bulimia and the hollow
nature of her marriage. By the end of the year,
his publishers claimed to have sold three million
copies in 23 languages, including Korean and
20 Icelandic, and it was estimated that Morton
would have made £3 million from the book.

Her success was not confined to pictures of
her or words written about her. When Diana
started to drive an Audi in 1994, the German car
25 giant, Volkswagen, saw sales rocket. A survey by
Majesty magazine three years ago calculated
that the Princess generated £14.5 million of free
publicity for products she bought.

Diana herself strove to use this phenomenal
30 attention to her own ends to promote the
charities and causes she was interested in. A
recent auction of her dresses in New York raised
£3.5 million for charity and it was rumoured that
the asking price to sit next to her at charity
35 dinners was as high as £100,000.

Glenda Cooper, *The Independent*, 1 September 1997

GLOSSARY

bulimia – a serious eating disorder
not confined to – not just about
revealed – showed

ACTIVITY

1 What do the following mean:
  a controversial interview
  b circulation leap
  c free publicity
  d phenomenal attention?
2 How much could Diana's photograph
  affect the sales of magazines and
  newspapers?
3 What other products sold more
  because they were linked with Diana?
4 In what ways was the princess used by
  the media like a 'good product'? In your
  own words, how do you think she felt
  about this?

Biggest television event in history

The funeral is expected to be the biggest television event in history and the BBC will make so much money from covering it and selling Diana-related programmes that it has decided to give all the money it makes to her memorial fund.

Estimates of a television audience of 2.5 billion are already being mentioned, but worldwide figures are notoriously difficult to estimate. Forty-five broadcasters have already requested a feed from the BBC's cameras in Westminster Abbey and along the funeral route.

In the biggest outside broadcast operation ever undertaken, 100 cameras and 300 technicians will cover the funeral in a simulcast for BBC1 and BBC2. BBC World, the corporation's international channel, will broadcast to a further 187 countries.

ITN and BBC are supplying pictures to two giant screens in Hyde Park for the crowds who cannot get to the funeral route.

BBC and ITN journalists are just a fraction of the number covering the funeral. The three big American networks, CNN, NBC and ABC, have brought an estimated 150 staff into London to provide coverage. The Foreign Press Association has registered 300 new journalists in London to cover

the funeral, but believes thousands more have not registered.

The total global audience is predicted to dwarf all previous events of this magnitude. Ironically, the wedding of Prince Charles and Diana captured a then record 700 million viewers.

Paul McCann,
The Independent,
4 September, 1997

ACTIVITY

1 How will the BBC make money from covering the funeral?

2 The report says the funeral will have a 'global audience'. What does this mean? Why was there so much interest in the funeral?

3 Why does the report mention the size of the TV audience for Charles and Diana's wedding?

EXTENDED ACTIVITY

4 Why was the funeral 'the biggest television event in history'? Use information from both reports in your answer. Also include these words:
- public interest
- royal family
- media hype
- tragic.

GLOSSARY

feed – a TV link

is predicted to dwarf – is expected to be bigger than

magnitude – size

notoriously difficult – very difficult

simulcast – simultaneous broadcast

That little madam over the road

Background

Here are two scenes from an episode of *Coronation Street* shown in October 1997. The script includes directions for the camera operators, as follows:

MS	medium shot
MW	medium wide
WS	wide shot
CU	close-up
MW3S	medium wide three (person) shot
2S	two (person) shot
MCU	medium close-up

Scene 2 (below) needs 3 cameras. These are labelled 1, 2 and 3. So the instruction:

<u>1 MS Martin, tilt to MCU Nick</u>

means 'Camera 1 starts with a medium shot of Martin, then moves on to a medium close-up of Nick.'

SCENE 2: Interior 0835AM

SET: Platts' Living Room

Martin, Gail, Nick, Sarah-Louise and David.
Nick, Sarah and David are at the table having breakfast while Martin and Gail are having theirs on the hoof.

<u>1 MS Martin tilt to MCU Nick</u>

Martin: You don't think you might be too late? Term must have started weeks ago.

Nick: I rang 'em yesterday. You can register any time till Christmas.

<u>2 MW3S</u>

Martin: Right.

Gail: And can you do a course just in PE?

Nick: (*Protests*) 'Just' ...? Oh, you think fitness isn't important? Health isn't important?

Martin: (*Not serious*) She asks some stupid questions ...

1 MCU Nick

Nick: (*Who is serious*) Sure, you can do a course in 'just PE.' That 'just' involves anatomy, physiology, sports injuries, study of different sports, sports facilities, physical education ...

2 MCU Martin

Martin: OK, OK, but what do you do in your second week?

3 WS

Nick: (*Not serious*) Fun-ney.

Gail: And you're saying they do this course at the local tech?

Nick: Local College of Further Education (*correcting Gail's Terminology*) And they do, yeah. Because I've asked them.

2 WS

Martin: Come on, David ... Sarah ... if you want a lift ... (*To Nick*) Give you one as well if you like.

1 MCU Nick

Nick: No, you're OK. I, er ... I'd rather walk.

Martin: Fair enough. And good luck. I hope they take you on.

Nick: Thanks.

3 2S Gail/Martin

Gail: (*Confides*) One good thing – it sounds like the kind of place where there's going to be lots of girls. Which should help to take his mind off that little madam over the road.

.... **ACTIVITIES** ....

1 What do the following camera directions mean:
MCU Sarah
MS Sarah to 2S with David?

2 What does 'having theirs on the hoof' mean?

3 How does Martin try to make fun of Nick's PE course?

4 How does Gail speak to Martin at the end of the scene? Comment on the director's use of Camera 3 at this point.

The camera directions for Scene 7 are not included.

SCENE 7: Interior 1100 AM

SET: College Coffee Bar

Nick, Leanne, College Students and Staff
The College Bar. We come to Nick and Leanne at a table with coffee and Leanne smoking. Both with lots of leaflets, forms etc, they've been given.

Nick: This seems a great place. Did you get the guided tour?
Leanne: (*Less easily impressed*) Looks a bit like a giant ladies' loo, our bit. 'Department of Hairdressing and Beauty Therapy.' Whatever beauty therapy is when it's at home.
Nick: (*Amused*) Let's see your timetable. (*Taking it from her*)
Leanne: I've got stuff practically every morning and afternoon. I said to her, I said hey, I'm only doing hairdressing – it says computers down here!
Nick: Apparently everyone has to do that.
Leanne: Mad. Why d'you want to know about computers to do somebody's hair? Anyway, listen, you fancy going into town?
Nick: (*Taken aback*) What, now?
Leanne: Yeah. Janice gave me some money.
Nick: But we've only just ... (*Gestures around him*) I mean we've got classes. Don't you have any classes today? (*Consults her timetable*) You do, yeah ...
Leanne: Supposed to have, but I acted all surprised. I said oh no, I can't start today, I have to go to the dentist. Me mam's made me an appointment. (*She thinks this is pretty clever. Nick is not so sure.*)
Nick: Yeah, but the reason I'm here – I want to do this course.
Leanne: So do what I'm doing. Start tomorrow.
Nick: I'm already starting late. I'm going to have to catch up as it is.

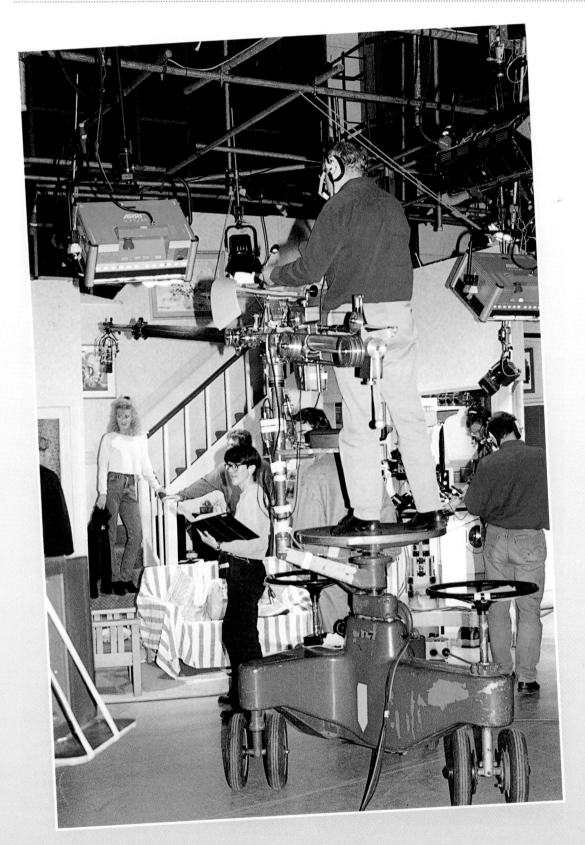

Leanne: (*Tuts*) Don't be so boring.

Nick: (*Dismayed*) Oh thanks.

Leanne: Well, y'are.

Nick: At least I know what I want to do. I thought you wanted to do hairdressing. 'Else why have you even bothered registering?

Leanne: Dunno. You said you were coming so I thought OK, come with you. So are we going or not?

Nick: (*In despair*) How can I when I've got classes? ...

Leanne: (*Leanne has had enough. She stands and collects her stuff together*) Yeah, yeah, I've heard it. OK, well, you do what you wanna do. I'll do what I wanna do.

Nick: (*Upset but isn't going to give way*) We can go into town after ...

Leanne: (*Looking at him pityingly*) I don't know what your Canadian girls were like. But over here you don't get second chances. At least not wi' me. (*She heads out of the door. Nick can only sit and watch her go.*)

ACTIVITY

1 Write camera directions for the start and end of this scene. Explain your choice of shots.
2 Close-up shots are only used at very tense, dramatic moments in the script. There are no close-ups in Scene 2. Why? Pick one part of Scene 7 where the director might have used a close-up, and say why.
3 How does Nick feel about Leanne? How does she feel about him?

EXTENDED ACTIVITY

4 Leanne and Nick meet again, later that day, outside Nick's house. Write down what they say to each other. Include directions for Nick and Leanne, as well as directions for two camera operators.
5 Prepare a rehearsed reading of your new scene.

111

MACBETH

Shakespeare: his life and times

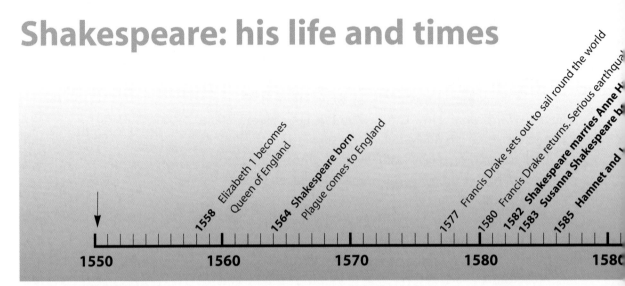

1558 Elizabeth 1 becomes Queen of England

1564 **Shakespeare born** Plague comes to England

1577 Francis Drake sets out to sail round the world

1580 Francis Drake returns. Serious earthqua

1582 **Shakespeare marries Anne H**

1583 **Susanna Shakespeare b**

1585 **Hamnet and**

1550   1560   1570   1580   1580

William Shakespeare
1564–1616

We know a lot about William Shakespeare the playwright and poet. His plays and poems have been read and performed all over the world for over two hundred years. But we know very little about Shakespeare the man.

He grew up in Stratford-upon-Avon. In the 16th century, Stratford was a small market town, surrounded by forests and fields. Shakespeare's father, John, was a glove-maker, and a wealthy man. His mother, Mary Arden, was also well-to-do. Her family owned a lot of farmland.

We know almost nothing about Shakespeare's childhood. He did go to school – nobody is sure which one – and learned Latin and Greek.

He married Anne Hathaway in 1582. They had three children. We know very little about Anne. We don't know if the marriage was a happy one. The children did not see much of their father. William was away from home for long periods. Everyone who knew him liked him. They describe him as a 'gentle man'.

The years 1585 to 1592 are sometimes called Shakespeare's 'lost years'. He left his wife and children in Stratford. Nobody knows where he went or what he did. He may have gone abroad, to Italy. Or he may have

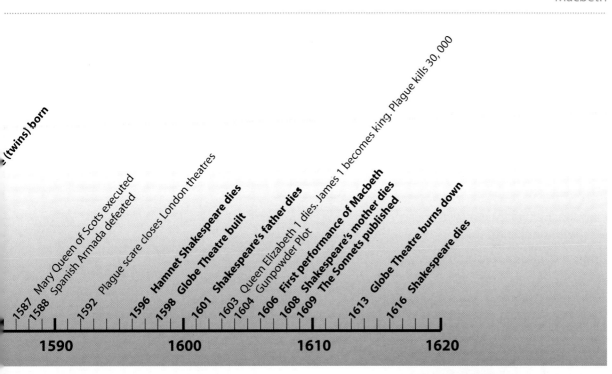

Timeline: (twins) born · 1587 Mary Queen of Scots executed · 1588 Spanish Armada defeated · 1592 Plague scare closes London theatres · 1596 Hamnet Shakespeare dies · 1598 Globe Theatre built · 1601 Shakespeare's father dies · 1603 Queen Elizabeth 1 dies, James 1 becomes king, Plague kills 30,000 · 1604 Gunpowder Plot · 1606 First performance of Macbeth · 1608 Shakespeare's mother dies · 1609 The Sonnets published · 1613 Globe Theatre burns down · 1616 Shakespeare dies

1590   1600   1610   1620

worked as a schoolteacher in England. In 1592, Shakespeare moved to London. He first made a name for himself as a poet. Then he concentrated on writing plays. Between 1594 and 1610, when he retired to Stratford, he wrote 37 plays.

He acted in many of his plays. He may have acted the ghost in Hamlet. He became part-owner of the Globe Theatre. When he retired, he was a very rich man.

From *Introducing Shakespeare*, by Paul Hicks and Angela Cairns, OUP Australia, 1995

The Globe Theatre.

ACTIVITY

1 Use information from the text and time-line to describe Shakespeare's childhood.
2 How old was he when he married and what do we know about his marriage?
3 Pick one event from the time-line and say how this might have affected Shakespeare's writing.

EXTENDED ACTIVITY

4 Did Shakespeare live 'a long and happy life'? Give reasons for your answer.

Macbeth: his road to ruin

Act 1

Macbeth meets the witches. They tell him he will be king.

Duncan declares Malcolm, his son, will be the next king.

Lady Macbeth wants to kill Duncan. Macbeth is not sure.

Duncan comes to Macbeth's castle.

Act 2

Macbeth murders Duncan.

He kills the guards, saying they killed the king.

Malcolm and Donalbain escape from Macbeth's castle.

Macbeth becomes king.

Act 3

Macbeth has Banquo killed.

Banquo's ghost appears at Macbeth's feast.

Macduff goes to England to get help to fight Macbeth.

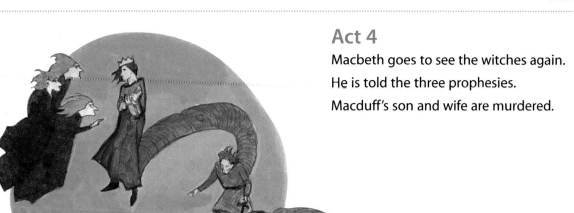

Act 4

Macbeth goes to see the witches again.

He is told the three prophesies.

Macduff's son and wife are murdered.

Act 5

Lady Macbeth sleepwalks.

She becomes ill.

Malcolm's army comes, disguised behind bushes.

Lady Macbeth dies.

Macduff kills Macbeth.

Malcolm is made king.

ACTIVITIES

1 What do the witches say about Macbeth's future?
2 Whose idea is it to murder King Duncan?
3 Who is blamed for the murder?
4 Why does Malcolm flee from Macbeth's castle?
5 Who is on Malcolm's side, against Macbeth?
6 Who comes back to haunt Macbeth?
7 How is Macbeth's rule ended?
8 Who takes the crown when Macbeth is dead?

EXTENDED ACTIVITY

9 Pick one scene from the play and summarize the main events in your own words. List the characters involved and say how Macbeth feels about each of them. Role play a conversation between two of the characters in this scene.

A lord and his lady

Macbeth

1 'For all's too weak for brave Macbeth.'
Captain, Act 1 Scene 2

2 'So foul and fair a day I have not seen.'
Macbeth, Act 1 Scene 3

3 'I have begun to plant thee, and will labour to make thee full of growing.'
Duncan, Act 1 Scene 4

4 'Stars, hide your fires, let not light see my black and deep desires.'
Macbeth, Act 1 Scene 4

ACTIVITY

1 Which quotation tells us that Macbeth:
  a felt ashamed of killing Duncan
  b was fearless in battle
  c had mixed feelings about the battle and what the future held
  d was well liked by the king?
2 Pick one of the quotations and say in your own words what else it tells us about the character of Macbeth.

GLOSSARY

hie – come
illness – madness, evil
thane – lord, chief

Lady Macbeth

1 'Thou wouldst be great, art not without
   ambition, but without the illness that
   should attend it.'
   Lady Macbeth, Act 1 Scene 5

2 'Hie thee hither, that I may pour my spirits in
   thine ear.'
   Lady Macbeth, Act 1 Scene 5

3 'Your face, my thane, is as a book
   where men may read strange matters.'
   Lady Macbeth, Act 1 Scene 5

4 'Give me the daggers. The sleeping and
   the dead are but pictures; 'tis the eye of
   childhood that fears a painted devil.'
   Lady Macbeth, Act 2 Scene 1

5 'Why do you make such faces? When
   all's done, you look but on a stool.'
   Lady Macbeth, Act 3 Scene 4

········· ACTIVITY ·········

1 Which quotation tell
us that Lady Macbeth
thinks Macbeth:
  a is tormented by
     childish fears
  b is not ruthless
     enough to be king
  c cannot hide his real
     feelings?
2 Why do you think
Lady Macbeth wants
to 'pour her spirits'
into Macbeth's ear?
Use one of the other
quotations to support
your answer.

·· EXTENDED ACTIVITY ··

3 Find one more short
speech in the play
which tells you about
the character of
Macbeth or Lady
Macbeth. Write it down
and say what it tells you
about that character.
Prepare a rehearsed
reading of the speech.

Thy blood is cold!

ACT 3 SCENE 4

The banqueting hall in the palace
Enter Macbeth, Lady Macbeth, Ross, Lennox, Lords, and attendants

Macbeth	You know your own degrees; sit down: at first and last,
	The hearty welcome.
Lords	Thanks to your majesty.
Macbeth	Ourself will mingle with society and play the humble host.
	Our hostess keeps her state, but in best time 5
	We will require her welcome.
Lady Macbeth	Pronounce it for me, sir, to all our friends;
	For my heart speaks they are welcome.

Enter First Murderer

Macbeth	See, they encounter thee with their hearts' thanks;	
	Both sides are even: here I'll sit i' the midst:	10
	Be large in mirth; anon, we'll drink a measure	
	The table round. (*He goes to the door*)	
	There's blood upon thy face.	
Murderer	'Tis Banquo's, then.	
Macbeth	'Tis better thee without than he within.	15
	Is he dispatch'd?	
Murderer	My lord, his throat is cut; that I did for him.	
Macbeth	Thou art the best o' the cut-throats;	
	Yet he's good that did the like for Fleance:	
	If thou didst it, thou art the nonpareil.	20
Murderer	Most royal sir, Fleance is 'scap'd.	
Macbeth:	Then comes my fit again: I had else been perfect;	
	Whole as the marble, founded as the rock,	
	As broad and general as the casing air:	
	But now I am cabin'd, cribb'd, confin'd, bound in	25
	To saucy doubts and fears. But Banquo's safe?	
First Murderer	Ay, my good lord; safe in a ditch he bides,	
	With twenty trenched gashes on his head,	
	The least a death to nature.	
Macbeth	Thanks for that.	30
	There the grown serpent lies: the worm that's fled	
	Hath nature that in time will venom breed,	
	No teeth for the present. Get thee gone; to-morrow	
	We'll hear ourselves again.	

Exit Murderer

.... **ACTIVITY** ....

1 How should Macbeth say the line 'There's blood upon thy face'?
   Give reasons for your answer.
2 What does this scene tell us about Banquo's death?
3 Role play a conversation between the first and second murderers after they have left Macbeth. What do they think of Macbeth?

Lady Macbeth	My royal lord,	35
	You do not give the cheer: the feast is sold	
	That is not often vouch'd, while 'tis a-making,	
	'Tis given with welcome: to feed were best at home;	
	From thence, the sauce to meat is ceremony,	
	Meeting were bare without it.	40
Macbeth	Sweet remembrancer!	
	Now good digestion wait on appetite,	
	And health on both!	
Lennox	May it please your highness sit.	

The Ghost of Banquo enters and sits in Macbeth's place

Macbeth	Here had we now our country's honour roof'd,	45
	Were the grac'd person of our Banquo present;	
	Who may I rather challenge for unkindness	
	Than pity for mischance!	
Ross	His absence, sir,	
	Lays blame upon his promise. Please't your highness	50
	To grace us with your royal company?	

Macbeth	The table's full.	
Lennox	Here is a place reserv'd, sir.	
Macbeth	Where?	
Lennox	Here, my good lord. What is't that moves your highness?	55
Macbeth	Which of you have done this?	
Lords	What, my good lord?	
Macbeth	Thou canst not say I did it; never shake	
	Thy gory locks at me.	
Ross	Gentlemen, rise; his highness is not well.	60
Lady Macbeth	Sit, worthy friends: my lord is often thus,	
	And hath been from his youth: pray you, keep seat;	
	The fit is momentary; upon a thought	
	He will again be well. If much you note him,	
	You shall offend him and extend his passion:	65
	Feed, and regard him not.	
	(Aside to Macbeth)Are you a man?	
Macbeth	Ay, and a bold one, that dare look on that	
	Which might appal the devil.	
Lady Macbeth	O proper stuff!	70
	This is the very painting of your fear;	
	This is the air-drawn dagger which, you said,	
	Led you to Duncan. O, these flaws and starts –	
	Impostors to true fear – would well become	
	A woman's story at a winter's fire,	75
	Authoriz'd by her grandam. Shame itself!	
	Why do you make such faces? When all's done,	
	You look but on a stool.	
Macbeth	Prithee, see there! Behold! look! lo! how say you?	
	(To Ghost) Why, what care I? If thou canst nod, speak too.	80
	If charnel-houses and our graves must send	
	Those that we bury back, our monuments	
	Shall be the maws of kites.	

Ghost disappears

ACTIVITY

1 Which lines tell us that Lennox cannot see Banquo's ghost?
2 Which lines tell us that Lady Macbeth cannot see it either?

Lady Macbeth	What! quite unmann'd in folly?	85
Macbeth	If I stand here, I saw him.	
Lady Macbeth	Fie, for shame!	
Macbeth	Blood hath been shed ere now, i' the olden time,	
	Ere human statute purg'd the gentle weal;	
	Ay, and since too, murders have been perform'd	
	Too terrible for the ear: the times have been	90
	That, when the brains were out, the man would die,	
	And there an end; but now they rise again,	
	With twenty mortal murders on their crowns,	
	And push us from our stools: this is more strange	
	Than such a murder is.	95
Lady Macbeth	My worthy lord,	
	Your noble friends do lack you.	
Macbeth	I do forget.	
	Do not muse at me, my most worthy friends;	
	I have a strange infirmity, which is nothing	100
	To those that know me. Come, love and health to all;	
	Then, I'll sit down. Give me some wine; fill full.	
	I drink to th' general joy of the whole table,	
	And to our dear friend Banquo, whom we miss;	
	Would he were here! to all, and him, we thirst,	105
	And all to all.	
Lords	Our duties, and the pledge.	

Enter Ghost

Macbeth	Avaunt! and quit my sight! Let the earth hide thee!	
	Thy bones are marrowless, thy blood is cold;	
	Thou hast no speculation in those eyes	110
	Which thou dost glare with.	

Lady Macbeth	Think of this, good peers,
	But as a thing of custom: 'tis no other;
	Only it spoils the pleasure of the time.
Macbeth	What man dare, I dare: 115
	Approach thou like the rugged Russian bear,
	The arm'd rhinoceros, or the Hyrcan tiger;
	Take any shape but that, and my firm nerves
	Shall never tremble: or be alive again,
	And dare me to the desert with thy sword; 120
	If trembling I inhabit then, protest me
	The baby of a girl. Hence, horrible shadow!
	Unreal mockery, hence!
	(Ghost vanishes)
	Why so; being gone,
	I am a man again. Pray you, sit still. 125
Lady Macbeth	You have displac'd the mirth, broke the good meeting,
	With most admir'd disorder.
Macbeth	Can such things be
	And overcome us like a summer's cloud,
	Without our special wonder? You make me strange 130
	Even to the disposition that I owe,
	When now I think you can behold such sights,
	And keep the natural ruby of your cheeks,
	When mine is blanch'd with fear.
Ross	What sights, my lord? 135
Lady Macbeth	I pray you, speak not; he grows worse and worse;
	Question enrages him. At once, good-night:
	Stand not upon the order of your going,
	But go at once.
Lennox	Good-night; and better health 140
	Attend his majesty!
Lady Macbeth	A kind good-night to all!

Exeunt Lords and Attendants

ACTIVITY

1 Why does Macbeth talk about 'twenty mortal murders on their crowns'?
2 Who is Macbeth talking to when he says: 'Let the earth hide thee'? Why does he say this?

Macbeth	It will have blood, they say; blood will have blood:
	Stones have been known to move and trees to speak;
	Augurs and understood relations have 145
	By maggot-pies, and choughs, and rooks, brought forth
	The secret'st man of blood. What is the night?
Lady Macbeth	Almost at odds with morning, which is which.
Macbeth	How sayst thou, that Macduff denies his person
	At our great bidding? 150
Lady Macbeth	Did you send to him, sir?
Macbeth	I hear it by the way; but I will send.
	There's not a one of them but in his house
	I keep a servant fee'd. I will to-morrow –
	And betimes I will – to the weird sisters: 155
	More shall they speak; for now I am bent to know,
	By the worst means, the worst. For mine own good
	All causes shall give way: I am in blood
	Stepp'd in so far, that, should I wade no more,
	Returning were as tedious as go o'er. 160
	Strange things I have in head that will to hand,
	Which must be acted ere they may be scann'd.
Lady Macbeth	You lack the season of all natures, sleep.
Macbeth	Come, we'll to sleep. My strange and self-abuse
	Is the initiate fear that wants hard use: 165
	We are yet but young in deed.

Exeunt

····················· **EXTENDED ACTIVITY** ·····················

1 Macbeth tells his wife, 'blood will have blood'. Blood is
   one of the most important images in this scene. Reread
   the scene. Find as many references to blood as you
   can. (Hint: some are not easy to spot!) Then describe a
   dream Macbeth had that night, after the banquet. Use
   images of blood in the dream and include Banquo and
   other characters from the play.
2 Retell the scene (or part of it) in modern English, and
   act it out.

Acknowledgements

The author and publisher are grateful for permission to reprint the following copyright material:

Advertising Standards Authority data and extract from report, by permission of the ASA.

W H Auden: 'As I Walked Out One Evening' from *Collected Poems*, by permission of the publishers, Faber & Faber Ltd.

Tony Bilbow and John Gau: King-Kong facts from *Lights, Camera, Action!* (Little Brown & Company (UK), 1995), by permission of the publishers.

Blackpool Borough Council Tourism, extracts from leaflets, by permission of the Borough Council.

British Broadcasting Corporation extract from news report, Radio 4's *Seven O'Clock News*, by permission of the BBC.

British Video Association extract from a 'Parents Guide to Video Classification' leaflet, by permission of the BVA.

Bill Bryson: extract from *Notes from a Small Island* (Black Swan, a division of Transworld Publishers Ltd, 1995), copyright Bill Bryson 1995, by permission of the publishers. All rights reserved.

Charles Causley: 'What Has Happened to Lulu?' from *Collected Poems* (Macmillan), by permission of David Higham Associates.

Channel Four News extract of report, copyright Independent Television News Ltd, 1997, by permission of ITN Channel Four News.

The Citizen Foundation, extracts from *Young Citizen's Passport* (Hodder & Stoughton Educational, 1996), by permission of Hodder & Stoughton Limited.

Louise Cook and Alan Snow: 'X-Ray Eyes' from *Alan Snow's Wacky Guide to Tricks and Illusions* (Walker, 1992), text copyright © 1992 Louise Cook, illustrations copyright © 1992 Alan Snow, by permission of the publishers Walker Books Ltd, London.

Wendy Cope: 'The Uncertainty of the Poet' from *Serious Concerns*, by permission of the publishers, Faber & Faber Ltd.

June Crebbin: 'Kite' from *The Jungle Sale* (Viking Kestrel, 1988), Copyright © June Crebbin 1988, by permission of the author.

The *Daily Mirror* articles by Carole Aye Maung, 'Oi, what are you looking at, dummy', *The Mirror*, 17.4.97; and by Geoffrey Lakeman, 'An arrow escape', *The Mirror*, 8.10.97, by permission of Mirror Syndication International.

The *Daily Telegraph* mini-sagas: 'Nemesis' by John Johns, 'Home is the sailor, home from the sea' by M Rumens, and 'A funny thing happened...' by Caroline L Appleby, from Brian Aldiss (ed): *Mini-sagas* (Sutton 1997), by permission of Ewan MacNaughton Associates on behalf of the Telegraph Group Ltd.

Julie Downing: extract from Cinderella, text © Hodder & Stoughton 1993, by permission of Hodder & Stoughton Limited.

Arthur Conan Doyle: 'Thirty Horse Power' from *How it Happened* (1918), copyright © 1996 by The Sir Arthur Conan Doyle Copyright Holders, by kind permission of Jonathan Clowes, Ltd, London, on behalf of Andrea Plunket, Administrator of the Sir Arthur Conan Doyle Copyrights.

The *Express*: text of article , 22 May 1997, by permission of Express Newspapers plc.

Neil Ferguson: extract from *English Weather* (1996), by permission of the publisher, Victor Gollancz Ltd.

Rachel Field: 'Skyscrapers' from *Taxis and Toadstools*, copyright 1924 by Yale University Press, published in the UK by William Heinemann (a division of Egmont Children's Books Ltd), by permission of Bantam Doubleday Dell Books for Young Readers and Egmont Children's Books Ltd.

Sarah Fiske: 'Flaming Valentine' first published here, Copyright © Sarah Fiske 1999, by permission of the author.

Geemarc Florida telephone specifications and photograph, by permission of Astral International Ltd.

Robert Graves: 'Love Without Hope' from *Collected Poems of Robert Graves*, by permission of the publishers, Carcanet Press Ltd.

The Guardian: extracts from article by Andrew Rawnsley, 7 March 1987, copyright © *The Guardian*, 1987, by permission of The Guardian.

Susan Hill: extract from *The Mist in the Mirror* (Mandarin, 1966), by permission of Random House UK Ltd.

The Independent: extracts from articles by Tania Alexander, 'European theme parks: a survival guide', The Independent on Sunday 6 April 1997; by Glenda Cooper, 'What will they do without her?', *The Independent* 1.9.97; and by Paul McCann, 'The biggest television event in history', *The Independent* 4.9.97; all by permission of Newspaper Publishing plc.

Independent Television Commission statistics from Television: The Public's View (1996), by permission of the ITC.

Andrew Johnston: 'How to Talk' from *How to Talk* (Victoria University Press, 1993) by permission of the publishers.

Jamaica Kincaid: 'Girl' from *At the Bottom of the River* (Farrar Straus & Giroux, 1984), © Jamaica Kincaid 1978, by permission of The Wylie Agency (UK) Ltd.

Anthony de Mello: 'The Golden Eagle' from *The Song of the Bird* (Gujarat Sahitya Prakash, 1982), by permission of the publishers.

Pat Moon: extract from *The Spying Game* (first published in the UK by Orchard Books, a division of the Watts Publishing Group, 1995), by permission of the publishers.

Jenny Morris: 'Dodo' first published in John Foster (ed): *Crack Another Yolk* (OUP, 1996), by permission of the author.

National Readership Survey data, by permission of the NRS.

National Society for the Prevention of Cruelty to Children, extract [with minor adaptations] from leaflet 'Screen Violence: what every parent should know', by permission of the NSPCC.

George Orwell: extract from *1984* (Secker & Warburg Ltd), copyright © George Orwell, 1949, by permission of A M Heath & Company Ltd on behalf of Mark Hamilton as the Literary Executor of the Estate of Sonia Brownell Orwell.

Louis Phillips: 'The Eraser Poem', first published in Willard S

Espy (ed): *A Children's Almanac of Words at Play* (Hodder & Stoughton), by permission of the author.

Carl Sandburg: 'The Auctioneer' from *Wind Song* by Carl Sandburg, copyright © 1986 by Margaret Sandburg, Janet Sandburg, and Helga Sandburg Crile, by permission of Harcourt Brace & Company.

William Shakespeare: Act 3 Scene 4 from *MacBeth*, Oxford School Shakespeare edition, by permission of Oxford University Press.

Idries Shah: slightly adapted version of 'The Indian Bird' from *The Way of the Sufi* by Idries Shah (Cape), by permission of Random House UK Ltd.

Alex Shearer: extract from opening of 'Getting a Life', first published here, copyright © Alex Shearer 1999, by permission of the author.

Sustrans Annual Review 1996, extracts reprinted by permission of Sustrans.

Dylan Thomas: extracts from 'Return Journey', a radio play, from *Quite Early One Morning* (Dent, 1954), by permission of David Higham Associates.

The Times facsimile of article 'Titanic Sunk' from *The Times*, 16 April 1912, copyright © Times Newspapers Limited 1912, by permission of Reuters Ltd and News International Syndication for The Times.

Venturer 121 telephone specifications and photograph, by permission of Venturer Electronics UK Ltd.

Peter Whalley: extracts from script for an episode of *Coronation Street*, by permission of the author and of Granada Television Ltd.

Martin Wyness: article 'If it feels right..', first published here, copyright © Martin Wyness 1999, by permission of the author.

Although every effort has been made to trace and contact copyright holders before publication this has not always been possible. If notified, the publisher will be pleased to rectify any errors or omissions at the earliest opportunity.

The publishers would like to thank the following for permission to reproduce photographs:

Allsport: p 24; Apex Photo Agency Ltd: p 28; Associated Press/Adrien Dennis: p 30; Astral Consumer Electronics Ltd: p 10 (right); Collections/Anthea Sieveking: p 44; Corbis Images: p 19 (middle); Corbis Images/Bettmann: pp 62, 67 (right); Corbis Images/Eye Ubiquitous/Paul Thompson: p 60 (top); Corbis Images/Chris Hellier: p 112; Corbis Images/Kurt Krieger: p 67 (bottom right); Corbis Images/UPI/Bettmann : p 34; Corbis Images/Patrick Ward: p 60 (bottom); Corel Corporation: pp 82, 86; Mary Evans Picture Library: p 113; Express Newspapers: p 32; Eye Ubiquitous/Yiogos Nikiteas: p 101; Format Photograpers/Pam Isherwood: p 100; Format Photographers/Mo Wilson: p 11 (right); Format Photographers/Lisa Woollett: p 11 (middle); Granada Television: pp 109, 110; The Independent Picture Syndication Service: p 105; The Kobal Collection: p 67 (top right); Lancashire County Library, Accrington Local Studies Library: p 8; Mattel UK Ltd: p 13 (right); Mirror Syndication Ltd: p 18; Parc Asterix: p 56; Popperfoto: p 35; Popperfoto/Blake Sell/Reuters: p 12; Popperfoto/Wendy Schwegmann: p 21; Port Aventura: p 57; Press Association:pp 20 (both), 29; Rex Features: p 106 (both); Sustrans Picture Library: 59; Topham Picturepoint/P.A. News/Fiona Hanson: p 33; Venturer Electronics UK Ltd: p 10 (left); Martin Wyness: pp 22, 23.

All other photographs are by Martin Sookias.

With thanks to: Virgin Megastore, Oxford; Denton's Cycles, Oxford; Jessica Whitaker; Megan and Georgia Rand; Paul Huzzey.